Maths Matters

Edco

Contents

Chapter		Strand	Page

Nice to be back!

Welcome back after the long summer holidays. You're now in third class and we hope that you have a very good year.

Here are a few easy questions to get you started.

1. How many months' holidays did you have? _____

2. Name the months. _____, _____

3. How many days in July? _____

4. How many days in August? _____

5. How many days is that altogether? _____

6. How many days in a week? _____

7. How many full weeks were in July? _____

8. How many full weeks were in August? _____

9. Did you or your friends have a birthday in July or August? _____ How many? _____

10. On what dates were the birthdays? _____

11. How many children are in your class? _____

12. How many girls? _____ How many boys? _____

13. Can you find out how many children are in the whole school this year? _____

Chapter 1
Place value

You need:
- hundreds, tens, and units
- notation boards
- to explain digit
- to use yellow for units and green for tens

Looking back

1. Write the numbers on these notation boards.

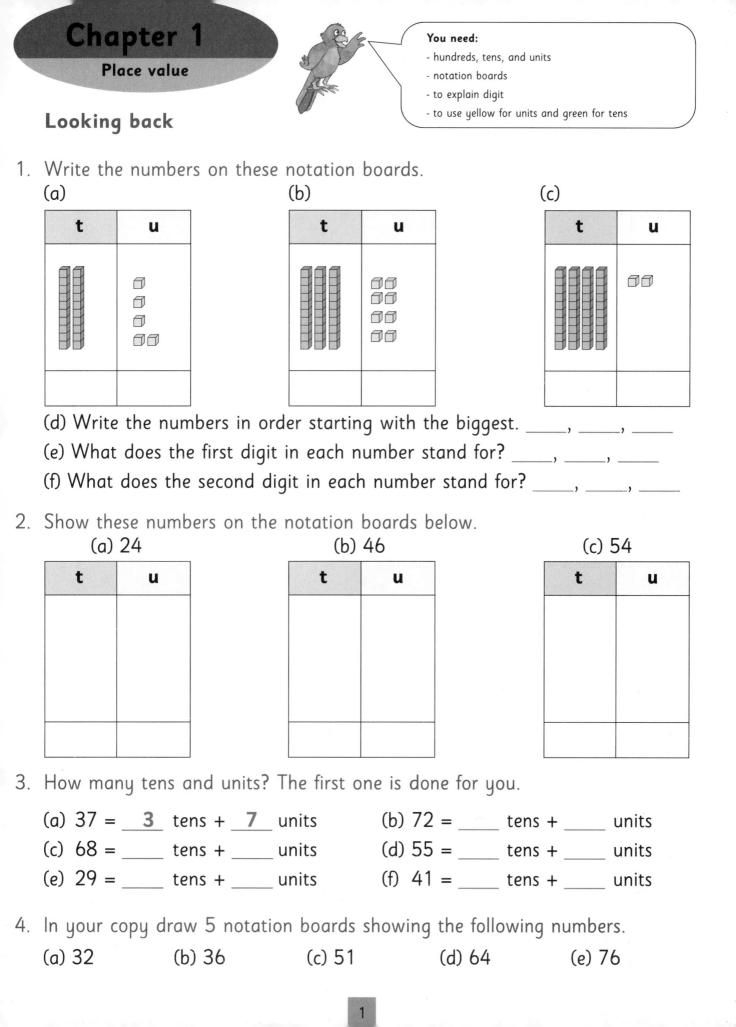

(a)

t	u

(b)

t	u

(c)

t	u

(d) Write the numbers in order starting with the biggest. _____, _____, _____

(e) What does the first digit in each number stand for? _____, _____, _____

(f) What does the second digit in each number stand for? _____, _____, _____

2. Show these numbers on the notation boards below.

(a) 24

t	u

(b) 46

t	u

(c) 54

t	u

3. How many tens and units? The first one is done for you.

   (a) 37 = __3__ tens + __7__ units   (b) 72 = ____ tens + ____ units
   (c) 68 = ____ tens + ____ units   (d) 55 = ____ tens + ____ units
   (e) 29 = ____ tens + ____ units   (f) 41 = ____ tens + ____ units

4. In your copy draw 5 notation boards showing the following numbers.
   (a) 32   (b) 36   (c) 51   (d) 64   (e) 76

Place value

1. Write the numbers shown on these abacuses.

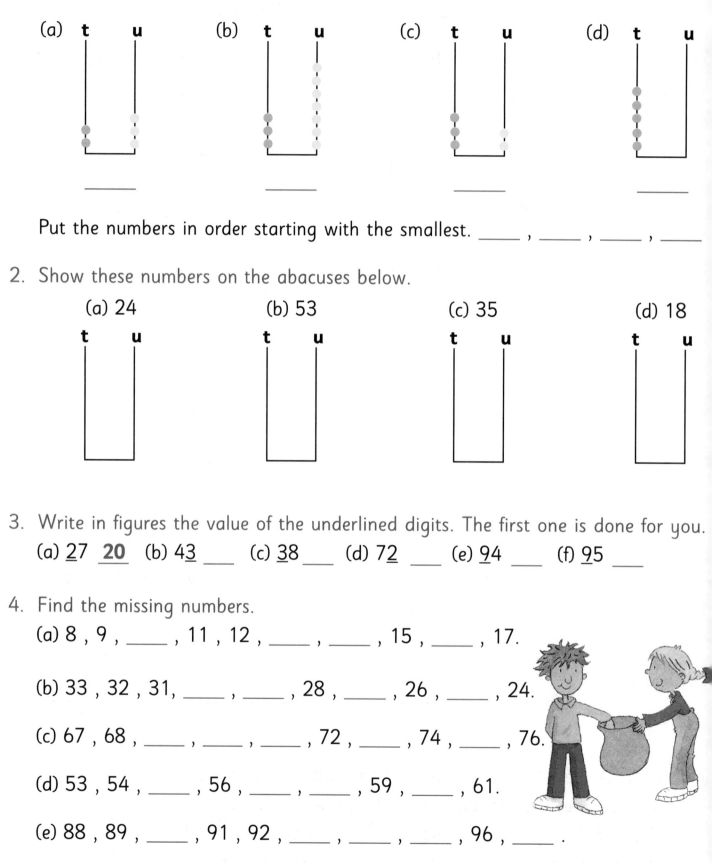

(a) t   u

(b) t   u

(c) t   u

(d) t   u

_____   _____   _____   _____

Put the numbers in order starting with the smallest. _____ , _____ , _____ , _____

2. Show these numbers on the abacuses below.

(a) 24   (b) 53   (c) 35   (d) 18

t   u   t   u   t   u   t   u

3. Write in figures the value of the underlined digits. The first one is done for you.

(a) 2̲7 **20**   (b) 4̲3 ____   (c) 3̲8 ____   (d) 7̲2 ____   (e) 9̲4 ____   (f) 9̲5 ____

4. Find the missing numbers.

(a) 8 , 9 , ____ , 11 , 12 , ____ , ____ , 15 , ____ , 17.

(b) 33 , 32 , 31, ____ , ____ , 28 , ____ , 26 , ____ , 24.

(c) 67 , 68 , ____ , ____ , ____ , 72 , ____ , 74 , ____ , 76.

(d) 53 , 54 , ____ , 56 , ____ , ____ , 59 , ____ , 61.

(e) 88 , 89 , ____ , 91 , 92 , ____ , ____ , ____ , 96 , ____ .

Place value

Moving on

1. The same number is shown in the 3 pictures. What number is it? _____

A

B

t   u

C

t	u
●	●
●	●
●	●
●	●
●	●
●	●
●	●
●	●
●	●

Now draw in another cube in picture **A** and colour it with your colouring pencil. What number have you now? _____
Is there a place for the new number in pictures **B** and **C**? _____

2. If you want to show numbers that are bigger than 99 on the abacus, you need to make a bigger abacus, like this:

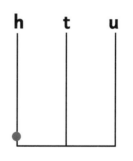

h   t   u

This is the number 100 (one hundred).
The one **red** counter stands for **one hundred**. There are no tens and no units.

3. Write the numbers shown on each abacus.

(a) **h**   t   u   (b) **h**   t   u   (c) **h**   t   u   (d) **h**   t   u

_____   _____   _____   _____

(e) Write the numbers in order starting with the smallest. ___ , ___ , ___ , ___
(f) What does the first digit in each number stand for?   ___ , ___ , ___ , ___
(g) What does the second digit in each number stand for? ___ , ___ , ___ , ___
(h) What does the third digit in each number stand for?   ___ , ___ , ___ , ___

Into the hundreds

1. Show these numbers on the abacuses below.

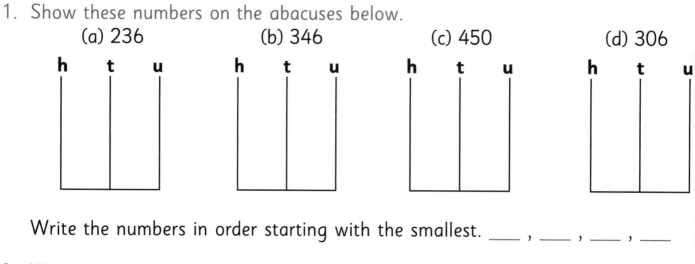

(a) 236   (b) 346   (c) 450   (d) 306

Write the numbers in order starting with the smallest. ____ , ____ , ____ , ____

2. Write in digits and words the values of the underlined digits.

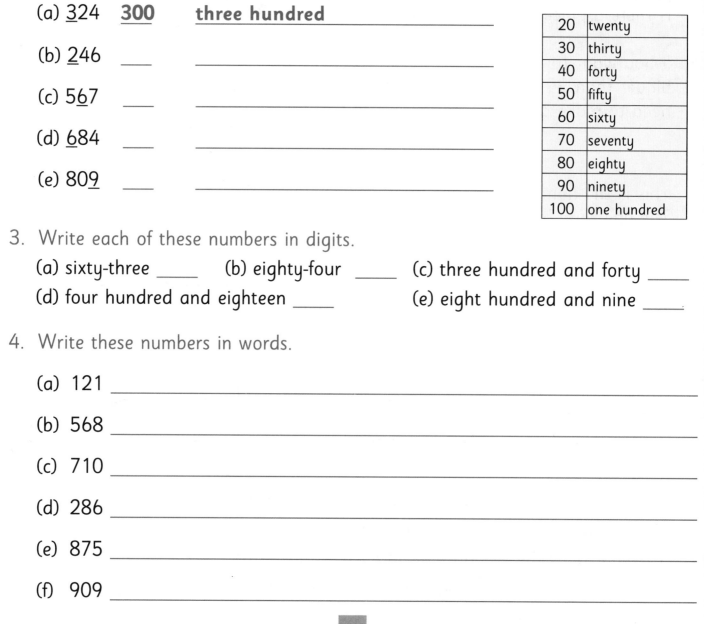

(a) 3̲24   **300**   **three hundred** _____

(b) 2̲46   ___   _____

(c) 56̲7   ___   _____

(d) 6̲84   ___   _____

(e) 80̲9   ___   _____

20	twenty
30	thirty
40	forty
50	fifty
60	sixty
70	seventy
80	eighty
90	ninety
100	one hundred

3. Write each of these numbers in digits.
   (a) sixty-three _____   (b) eighty-four _____   (c) three hundred and forty _____
   (d) four hundred and eighteen _____   (e) eight hundred and nine _____

4. Write these numbers in words.

   (a) 121 _____

   (b) 568 _____

   (c) 710 _____

   (d) 286 _____

   (e) 875 _____

   (f) 909 _____

More hundreds

1. Add 10 to the following numbers.
   (a) 26 ____ (b) 47 ____ (c) 99 ____ (d) 209 ____ (e) 930 ____ (f) 989 ____

2. How many hundreds, tens and units in each of these amounts?
   (a) 176 = __1__ hundred, __7__ tens and __6__ units
   (b) 298 = ___ hundreds, ___ tens and ___ units
   (c) 721 = ___ hundreds, ___ tens and ___ units
   (d) 905 = ___ hundreds, ___ tens and ___ units

3. Add 100 to the following numbers.
   (a) 17____ (b) 7____ (c) 36____ (d) 84____ (e) 99____ (f) 101____
   (g) 211____ (h) 301____ (i) 410____ (j) 735____ (k) 790____ (l) 899____

4. Each of these balloons contains three digits. Use these digits to make
   the biggest number possible. The first one is done for you.

843							

5. Starting with the **smallest**, write these numbers in the top row of this grid.
   Write the letter that is with each number underneath it, in the bottom row.
   You will find a short sentence.

   310 **(G)**   702 **(A)**   999 **(S)**   499 **(D)**   222 **(M)**   576 **(T)**   107 **(I)**
   926 **(H)**   375 **(O)**   136 **(A)**   816 **(T)**   641 **(M)**   427 **(O)**   512 **(A)**

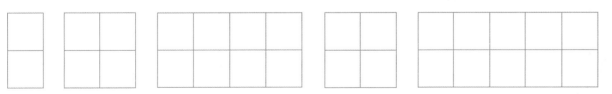

Rounding to the nearest 10

1.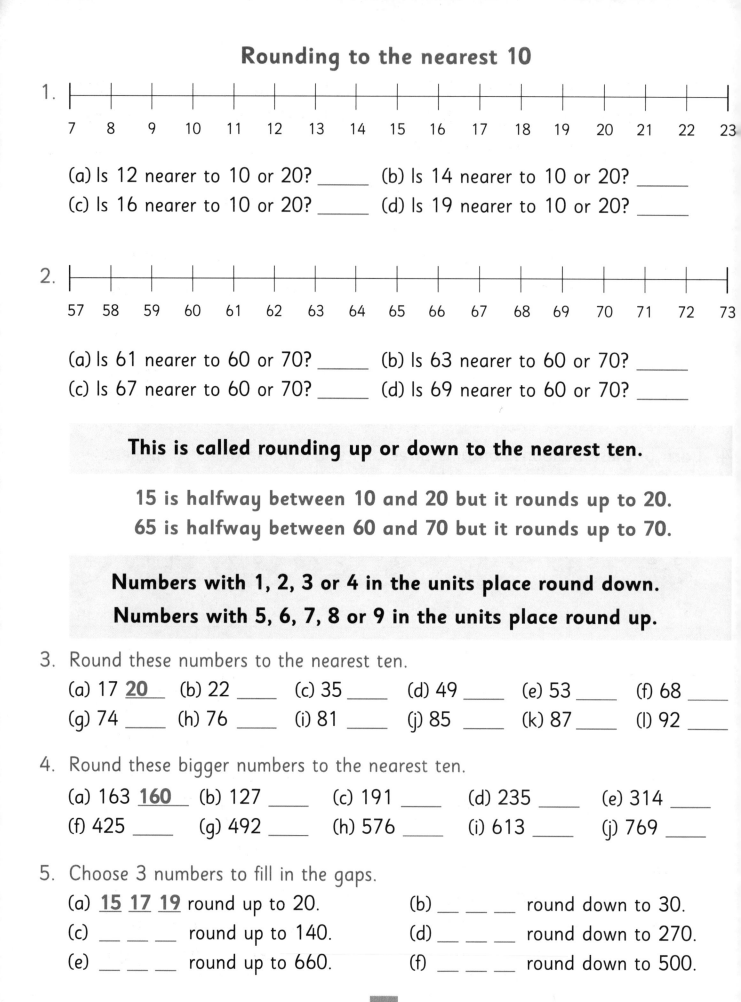

7 8 9 10 11 12 13 14 15 16 17 18 19 20 21 22 23

(a) Is 12 nearer to 10 or 20? _____ (b) Is 14 nearer to 10 or 20? _____
(c) Is 16 nearer to 10 or 20? _____ (d) Is 19 nearer to 10 or 20? _____

2.

57 58 59 60 61 62 63 64 65 66 67 68 69 70 71 72 73

(a) Is 61 nearer to 60 or 70? _____ (b) Is 63 nearer to 60 or 70? _____
(c) Is 67 nearer to 60 or 70? _____ (d) Is 69 nearer to 60 or 70? _____

This is called rounding up or down to the nearest ten.

15 is halfway between 10 and 20 but it rounds up to 20.
65 is halfway between 60 and 70 but it rounds up to 70.

Numbers with 1, 2, 3 or 4 in the units place round down.
Numbers with 5, 6, 7, 8 or 9 in the units place round up.

3. Round these numbers to the nearest ten.
   (a) 17 **20** (b) 22 ____ (c) 35 ____ (d) 49 ____ (e) 53 ____ (f) 68 ____
   (g) 74 ____ (h) 76 ____ (i) 81 ____ (j) 85 ____ (k) 87 ____ (l) 92 ____

4. Round these bigger numbers to the nearest ten.
   (a) 163 **160** (b) 127 ____ (c) 191 ____ (d) 235 ____ (e) 314 ____
   (f) 425 ____ (g) 492 ____ (h) 576 ____ (i) 613 ____ (j) 769 ____

5. Choose 3 numbers to fill in the gaps.
   (a) **15 17 19** round up to 20.   (b) __ __ __ round down to 30.
   (c) __ __ __ round up to 140.   (d) __ __ __ round down to 270.
   (e) __ __ __ round up to 660.   (f) __ __ __ round down to 500.

Rounding to the nearest 100

1. (a) Is 286 nearer to 200 or 300? _____ (b) Is 217 nearer to 200 or 300?_____

   (c) Is 341 nearer to 300 or 400? _____ (d) Is 327 nearer to 300 or 400?_____

   (e) Is 509 nearer to 500 or 600? _____ (f) Is 862 nearer to 800 or 900? _____

This is called rounding up or down to the nearest hundred.

Numbers with 1, 2, 3 or 4 in the tens place round down.

Numbers with 5, 6, 7, 8 or 9 in the tens place round up.

2. Round these numbers to the nearest hundred.

   (a) 156 _____ (b) 127 _____ (c) 186 _____ (d) 149 _____ (e) 171 _____

   (f) 219 _____ (g) 336 _____ (h) 476 _____ (i) 489 _____ (j) 315 _____

   (k) 526 _____ (l) 562 _____ (m) 696 _____ (n) 638 _____ (o) 674 _____

   (p) 754 _____ (q) 817 _____ (r) 851 _____ (s) 898 _____ (t) 949 _____

3. Round these numbers to the nearest 10 and then to the nearest 100.

   (a) 63 **60   100**   (b) 75 _____ _____   (c) 57 _____ _____

   (d) 123 _____ _____   (e) 167 _____ _____   (f) 215 _____ _____

   (g) 711 _____ _____   (h) 892 _____ _____   (i) 545 _____ _____

4. (a) Round up or down to the
      nearest ten.

8 5	10
15 19	20
29 31	30
44 47	40
52 59	50
65 72	60
77 83	70
85 94	80
92 89	90

   (b) Round up or down to the
      nearest hundred.

51 98	100
102 151	200
163 250	300
256 350	400
371 450	
489 550	500
590 649	600
699	700
763 817	800
850 899	900

Gone fishing

Paul went fishing without permission. His mother was very annoyed, and when he arrived home she asked him, 'Where were you?'

Paul said, 'I went fishing.'

'If you wanted to go fishing,' said his mother, 'why didn't you come and ask me first?'

Paul answered ? ? ? ? ? ? ? ? ?'

Write these numbers in order, starting with the **smallest**, in the top row of the grid. Write the letter that is with each number underneath it in the bottom row. When you have finished, you will find out what Paul said to his mother.

739 **(H)**   374 **(E)**   121 **(S)**   594 **(F)**   112 **(U)**   640 **(S)**   409 **(T)**
89 **(C)**   816 **(I)**   22 **(E)**   910 **(G)**   291 **(N)**   16 **(B)**   901 **(N)**
210 **(I)**   567 **(O)**   497 **(G)**   180 **(E)**   347 **(T)**   108 **(A)**   219 **(W)**
479 **(O)**   604 **(I)**   271 **(A)**   390 **(D)**

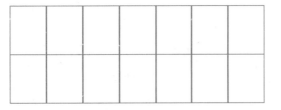
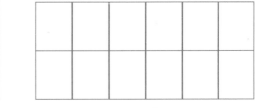

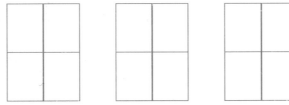
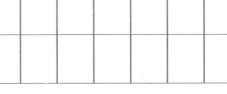

You need:
- hundreds, tens and units
- notation boards
- use red for hundreds, green for tens and yellow for units

Looking back

1. (a) 2 + 5 = ____   (b) 3 + 7 = ____   (c) 8 + 4 = ____
   (d) 10 + 8 = ____   (e) 14 + 5 = ____   (f) 18 + 10 = ____

2. (a) 3 + 2 + 5 = ____   (b) 4 + 6 + 8 = ____   (c) 3 + 9 + 9 = ____
   (d) 4 + 6 + 10 = ____   (e) 9 + 1 + 5 = ____   (f) 8 + 7 + 5 = ____

3.

t	u
+	
5	9

Add 34 and 25.

Step 1
Add the units.
```
 tu
 34
+25
  9
```

Step 2
Add the tens.
```
 tu
 34
+25
 59
```
Answer: 59

4. (a) tu   (b) tu   (c) tu   (d) tu   (e) tu   (f) tu
       23   56   41   34   42   53
     + 42   + 32   + 27   + 30   + 26   + 36
     ____   ____   ____   ____   ____   ____

5.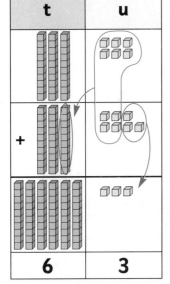

t	u
+	
6	3

Add 36 and 27.

Step 1
Add the units and bring the ten to the tens place.
```
 t u
 3 6
+2₁7
   3
```

Step 2
Now add the tens.
```
 t u
 3 6
+2₁7
 6 3
```
Answer: 63

Looking back

1.

t	u

+	

Add 28 and 53 (finish the picture yourself).

Step 1
Add the units and bring the ten to the tens place.

```
  t u
  2 8
+ 5 3
_____
```

Step 2
Now add the tens.

```
  t u
  2 8
+ 5 3
_____
```

Answer: _____

2. (a)
```
  t u
  4 6
+ 1 8
_____

_____
```
(b)
```
  t u
  3 7
+ 2 6
_____

_____
```
(c)
```
  t u
  4 8
+ 2 5
_____

_____
```
(d)
```
  t u
  3 7
+ 3 5
_____

_____
```
(e)
```
  t u
  4 9
+ 2 2
_____

_____
```
(f)
```
  t u
  4 5
+ 2 7
_____

_____
```

3. There are 27 children in third class and 28 in fourth class. How many children altogether in the two classes? _____

4.  Jason has 35c. Sharon has 28c more than him. How much money has Sharon? _____

5. Martha got €25 for her birthday. Mary got €20 more than her. How much altogether have the two girls? _____

Bigger numbers

Moving on

1. Add 168 and 145.

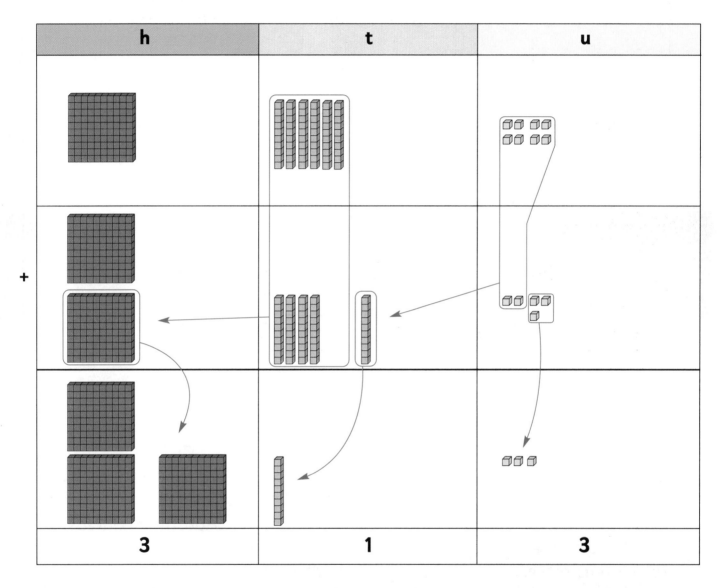

h	t	u
3	**1**	**3**

Step 1
Add the units
and bring the ten
to the tens place.

```
  h t u
  1 6 8
+ 1 4⁵5
      3
```

Step 2
Add the tens
and bring the hundred
to the hundreds place.

```
  h t u
  1 6 8
+ 1¹4⁵5
    1 3
```

Step 3
Add the hundreds.

```
  h t u
  1 6 8
+ 1¹4⁵5
  3 1 3
```

Bigger numbers

1. Add 236 and 175. Use the example on the previous page to help you.

h	t	u
+		

Step 1
Add the units
and bring the ten
to the tens place.

    h t u
    2 3 6
  + 1 7 5
  _____

Step 2
Add the tens
and bring the hundred
to the hundreds place.

    h t u
    2 3 6
  + 1 7 5
  _____

Step 3
Add the hundreds.

    h t u
    2 3 6
  + 1 7 5
  _____

2. Now try these.

(a) h t u
      2 3 6
    + 1 4 5
    _____

(b) h t u
      1 4 8
    + 3 3 9
    _____

(c) h t u
      2 4 6
    + 1 4 8
    _____

(d) h t u
      1 5 7
    + 1 4 8
    _____

(e) h t u
      3 4 6
    + 2 3 8
    _____

(f) h t u
      2 5 6
    + 4 3 9
    _____

Bigger numbers

1.
(a)
h t u
3 9 6
2 8 4
+   6 8
———

(b)
h t u
4 5 6
2 9 8
+   7 4
———

(c)
h t u
2 4 8
  9 6
+ 1 8 4
———

(d)
h t u
5 2 7
  4 8
+ 1 2 9
———

(e)
h t u
3 9 6
2 4 8
+   8
———

(f)
h t u
4 5 6
2 9 8
+   7
———

2. (a) 198 + 186 + 247 = ____   (b) 496 + 278 + 135 = ____

(c) 437 + 245 + 186 = ____   (d) 395 + 169 + 248 = ____

(e) 298 + 184 + 67   = ____   (f) 495 + 245 + 63   = ____

(g) 498 +   7   + 64   = ____   (h) 298 +   45 + 7   = ____

3. Alan has 35c and Ryan has 45c.
How much have they got all together? ____

4.  The children in third and fourth class went on a school tour. There were 29 children in third class and 33 in fourth class. Four parents also went with the 2 teachers. **How many were on the bus?** ____ (Don't forget the driver!)

5. There were 58 people on board the train. When it stopped at the station, 48 more people boarded. **How many passengers were on the train altogether when it left the station?** ____

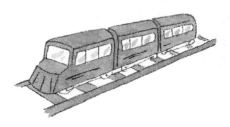

6.  Paula had 78 stamps and Martin had 29 more than that. **How many stamps did Martin have?**
____

Fun and games

1.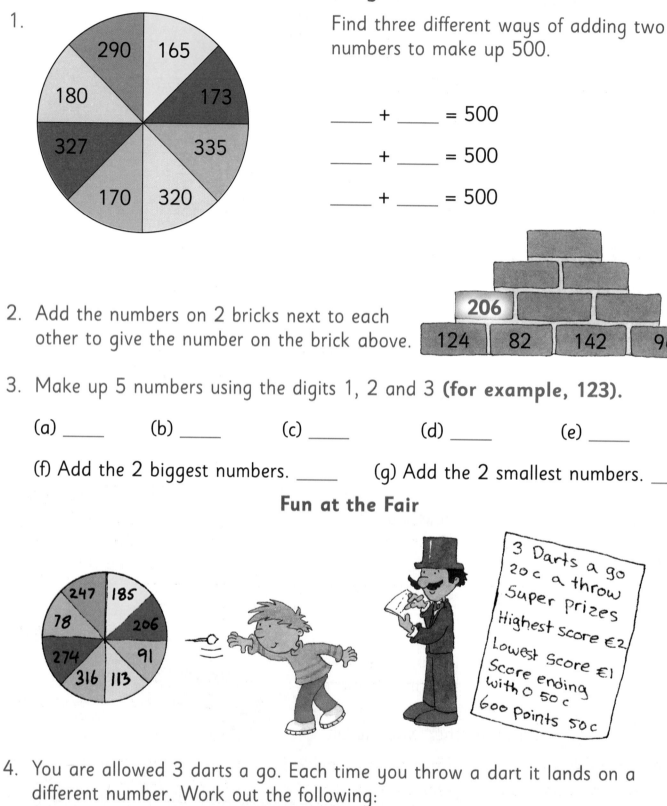

Find three different ways of adding two numbers to make up 500.

____ + ____ = 500

____ + ____ = 500

____ + ____ = 500

2. Add the numbers on 2 bricks next to each other to give the number on the brick above.

206

124   82   142   96

3. Make up 5 numbers using the digits 1, 2 and 3 (for example, 123).

(a) ____   (b) ____   (c) ____   (d) ____   (e) ____

(f) Add the 2 biggest numbers. ____   (g) Add the 2 smallest numbers. ____

Fun at the Fair

247 185
78   206
274   91
316 113

3 Darts a go
20c a throw
Super prizes
Highest score €2
Lowest Score €1
Score ending
with 0 50c
600 points 50c

4. You are allowed 3 darts a go. Each time you throw a dart it lands on a different number. Work out the following:
   (a) the highest possible score ____   (b) the lowest possible score ____
   (c) the 3 numbers that add up to 600 ____ + ____ + ____ = 600
   (d) 3 other numbers that give a different score ending with 0
       ____ + ____ + ____ = ____

You need:
- hundreds, tens and units
- numeral cards 0 to 9
- to use the appropriate colours for hundreds, tens and units
- colouring pencils/markers
- notation boards
- to practise subtraction facts

Looking back

1. (a) 5 – 2 = _____   (b) 7 – 3 = _____   (c) 9 – 4 = _____
   (d) 8 – 5 = _____   (e) 6 – 2 = _____   (f) 7 – 7 = _____

2. (a) 14 – 3 = _____   (b) 17 – 6 = _____   (c) 15 – 4 = _____
   (d) 19 – 7 = _____   (e) 18 – 8 = _____   (f) 19 – 4 = _____

3. (a) 20 – 7 = _____   (b) 22 – 8 = _____   (c) 23 – 6 = _____
   (d) 24 – 18 = _____ (e) 25 – 15 = _____ (f) 28 – 19 = _____

4. From 62 take 25 (or 62 – 25).

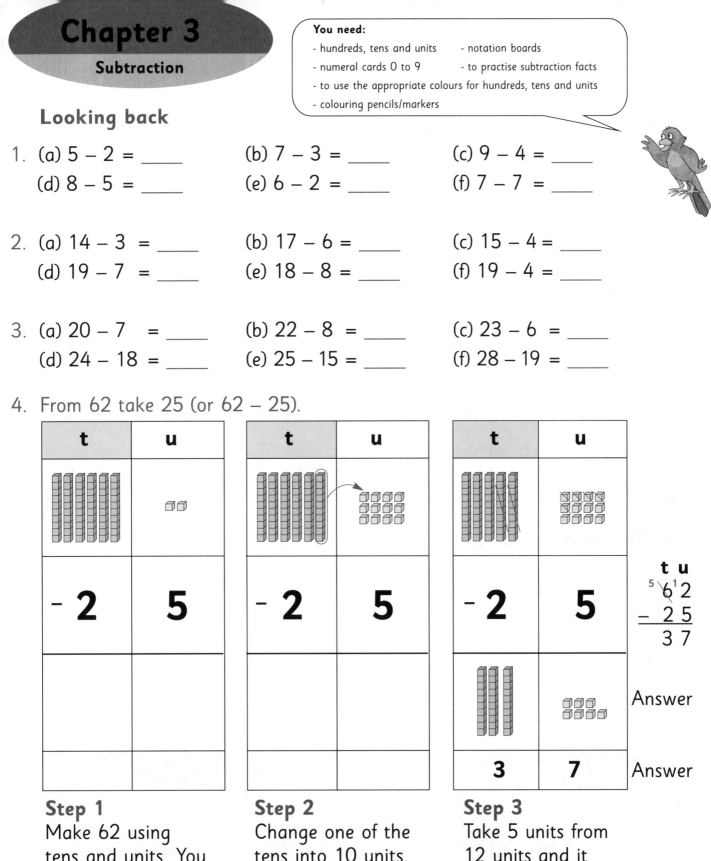

Step 1
Make 62 using tens and units. You have to take 25 away from 62. But you cannot take 5 units from 2 units.

Step 2
Change one of the tens into 10 units. Now you have 5 tens and 12 units.

Step 3
Take 5 units from 12 units and it leaves 7 units. Then take 2 tens from 5 tens and it leaves 3 tens.

Subtraction for you

1. Take 18 from 43 (or 43 – 18).

t	u
- 1	8

t	u
- 1	8

t	u
- 1	8
2	5

Short way:
$$\overset{3}{\cancel{4}}{}^{1}3$$
$$-18$$

Answer

Answer

2. Use your own class notation board and numerals 1 to 9 to do these.

    (a) 32 – 16 = ___   (b) 31 – 14 = ___   (c) 43 – 25 = ___   (d) 44 – 27 = ___

3. (a)   51   (b)   63   (c)   41   (d)   73   (e)   42   (f)   53
       – 26   – 24   – 27   – 28   – 26   – 36
       ____   ____   ____   ____   ____   ____

4. St Michael's school has 92 pupils. Every Tuesday 28 of them go to the swimming pool. How many are left in the school? _____

5.

How many would be left in a school of 80 if 56 of them went on a school trip? _____

6. Lisa had 80c. She spent 36c on a drink for her lunch. How much had she left? ____

Take-away stories

Here are 4 take-away questions with the answers.
Make up a story and draw a picture for each of them.
(a) 32 – 16 = 16 (b) 52 – 15 = 37 (c) 64 – 40 = 24 (d) 90 – 72 = 18

Story:_____

_____

_____

_____

_____

Story:_____

_____

_____

_____

_____

Story:_____

_____

_____

_____

Story:_____

_____

_____

_____

Bigger numbers

Moving on

1. From 343 take 157 (343 – 157).

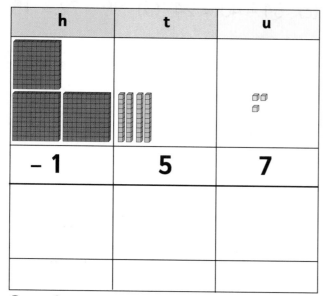

Step 1

Make 343 using hundreds, tens and units. You have to take 157 from 343. But you cannot take 7 units from 3 units.

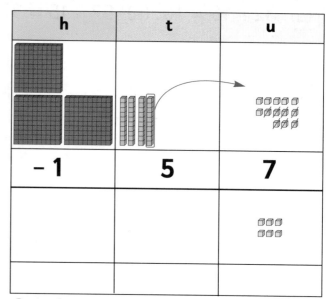

Step 2

Change one of the tens into 10 units. You now have 3 hundreds, 3 tens and 13 units. Take 7 away from 13. This leaves 6. Put the 6 units in the answer slot.

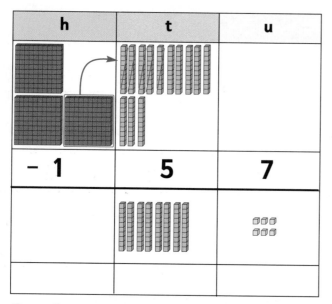

Step 3

You cannot take 5 tens from 3 tens. Change one of the hundreds into 10 tens. Take 5 tens from 13 tens. This leaves 8 tens. Put the 8 tens in the answer slot.

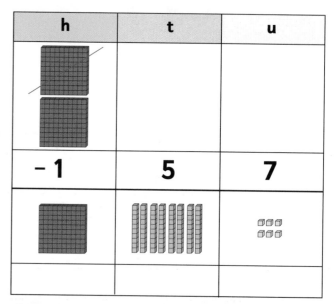

Step 4

Take 1 hundred from 2 hundreds. This leaves 1 hundred. Put the 1 hundred in the answer slot. What is the answer?

Bigger numbers

1. Try these, using your notation board. Then do them the short way.

(a) 345
  − 129

(b) 465
  − 229

(c) 392
  − 146

(d) 584
  − 326

(e) 462
  − 238

(f) 583
  − 247

(g) 763
  − 249

(h) 862
  − 438
-----

2. Now do these.

(a) 512
  − 165

(b) 324
  − 167

(c) 512
  − 146

(d) 723
  − 168

(e) 632
  − 368

(f) 745
  − 287

(g) 756
  − 479

(h) 824
  − 536
-----

3. From 300 take 168 (300 − 168).

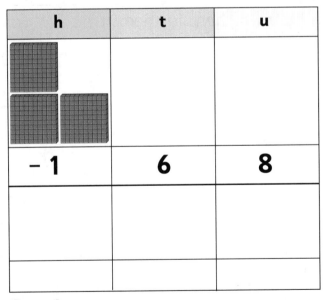

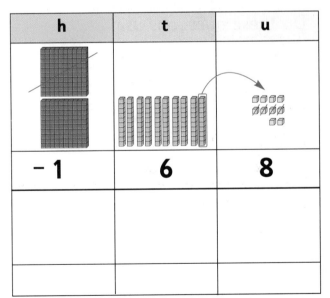

Step 1

Make 3 hundreds. You have to take 168 from 300 but you cannot take 8 from nothing. There are no tens so change one of the hundreds into 10 tens.

Step 2

Change one of the tens into 10 units. Take away 8 units, 6 tens and 1 hundred. Write what is left in the answer slot.

Using notation boards

1. Take 174 from 400 (or 400 − 174).

h	t	u
−		

h	t	u
−		

2. Do these questions using your notation board.   Then do them the short way.

(a)   300
    − 156
    ――――

(b)   200
    − 74
    ――――

(c)   300
    − 148
    ――――

(d)   400
    − 256
    ――――

(e)   400
    − 346
    ――――

(f)   500
    − 299
    ――――

(g)   700
    − 374
    ――――

(h)   600
    − 432
    ――――

(i)   800
    − 642
    ――――

(j)   900
    − 204
    ――――

3. These questions are written in a different way. In your copy do them the short way.

(a) 432 − 256   (b) 649 − 189   (c) 512 − 376   (d) 740 − 296

(e) 601 − 496   (f) 710 − 395   (g) 800 − 567   (h) 900 − 742

Problems for you to solve

1.  There are 252 children attending Greenfield School. Last Friday there were 68 absent. How many were in attendance? _____

2. There are 372 gardaí in Pearse Street Garda Station. 149 of them are on night duty. **How many are on day duty?** _____

3.  The principal of Kilmore School bought 288 pencils for the school shop after the summer holidays. When Christmas came she had 99 left. **How many did she sell?** _____

4. Ross has 82c. Paul has 28c less than him. **How much has Paul?** _____

5.  Sinéad is 9 years of age. Her grandmother is 66 years. **What is the difference in their ages?** _____ years

In this number wall, find the **difference** between 2 bricks to get the one above. One of them has been done for you.

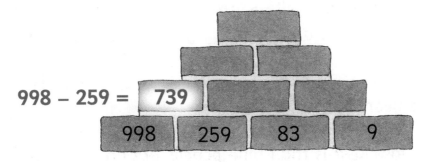

998 − 259 = 739

| 998 | 259 | 83 | 9 |

During the summer holidays Mrs Brown counted the number of items she had in the shop. Answer the following questions:

1. How many pencils altogether in the shop? _____

2. What is the total number of erasers? _____

3. How many more blue biros than red biros are there? _____

4. Mrs Brown estimates that she will need 400 maths copies for the year. **How many more does she need to order?** _____

5. She bought 800 writing copies at the beginning of last year. **How many did she sell during the year?** _____

6. How many less yellow pencils than blue pencils are on the shelf? _____

7. How many more plastic sharpeners than metal sharpeners has Mrs Brown? _____

8. She bought a box of 144 pencil/ink erasers. **How many did she sell during the year?** _____

9. Write a question about the shop with the following number sentence:
125 – 78 = 47 _____

_____

10. Find the missing number in this addition sentence and then write the story.
225 + _____ = 393 _____

_____

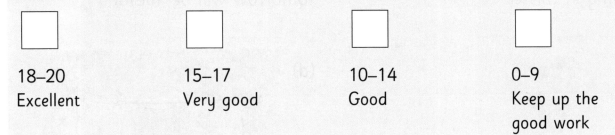

How well did you do?

Give yourself 2 marks for each question you answered correctly
and then tick the box with your score.

☐ 18–20
Excellent

☐ 15–17
Very good

☐ 10–14
Good

☐ 0–9
Keep up the
good work

You need: - coloured counters
- 2 dice for each group
- non-see-through bags
- colouring pencils

1. Look at these three pictures and discuss the word under each one.

This box contains chocolates.

| possible |

This box contains a pair of shoes.

| certain |

This box contains a herd of live elephants.

| impossible |

2. Now discuss what you see in the following pictures and choose which of the following words goes under each one: | possible | | certain | | impossible |

(a)

The baby will now drive Mammy in this car.

(b)

If today is Monday, then tomorrow will be Tuesday.

(c)

Martin will spill his drink.

(d)

The clothes will be dry in 2 minutes.

(e)

If it is 4 o'clock now then it will be 5 o'clock in an hour.

(f)

Mr Smith will buy a book.

Likely or unlikely

1. Discuss what you see in these two pictures and discuss the word under each one.

The children will go for a swim.

| likely |

The children will go for a swim.

| unlikely |

2. Now look at these pictures and read the sentence under each one. Choose which of the following words goes under each one: | likely | unlikely |

(a)

Amy is going to school.

| |

(b)

Mr Burke will wear a Spiderman suit to school tomorrow.

| |

(c)

John will win the race.

| |

(d)

Some cards will fall.

| |

(e)

The phone will ring today.

| |

(f)

A famous film star will come to Claire's party.

| |

Time to choose

1. Put 5 counters of one colour and 5 counters of another colour in a bag that you cannot see through. You will have six chances, picking out one counter each time. You must replace the counter each time before you pick again. Colour the boxes to show how many of each colour you think you will pick out.

    My Guess

1	2	3	4	5	6

    Now ask a friend to hold the bag while you choose your counters. Record the results below by colouring the boxes.

    Actual Results

1	2	3	4	5	6

    Discuss the results.

    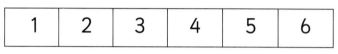

2. This time put 3 counters of one colour and 7 counters of another colour in the bag. Do you think the results are likely to be different if you play the same game with these counters? _____ Why? _____

    _____

    My Guess

1	2	3	4	5	6

    Now play the game and record the results.

    Actual Results

1	2	3	4	5	6

    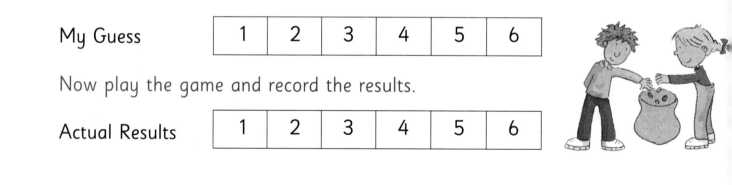

3. Play again with 1 counter of one colour and 9 counters of another colour. Discuss the possible result before you play.

    My Guess

1	2	3	4	5	6

    Actual Results

1	2	3	4	5	6

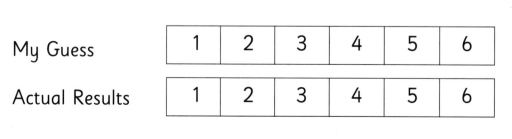

Roll the dice

Look closely at the number of dots on the faces of a dice. Read these questions carefully and experiment with one or two dice before you choose one of the following words: possible   impossible   certain

Using 1 dice

1. When I roll the dice once I will score 6. [ ]

2. I may score 7 if I roll the dice once. [ ]

3. When I roll the dice twice and add my scores I will have scored at least 2. [ ]

4. When I roll the dice 3 times and add my scores I might have scored 19. [ ]

5. After 3 rolls, I will have scored less than 3. [ ]

6. If I roll the dice 5 times and add my scores, I will have scored 5 or more. [ ]

7. Four rolls of the dice might give me a score of 25. [ ]

Using 2 dice

8. When I roll the two dice once I will have a score of at least 2. [ ]

9. One roll of the two dice may give me a score of 12. [ ]

10. I scored 15 on one roll of the two dice. [ ]

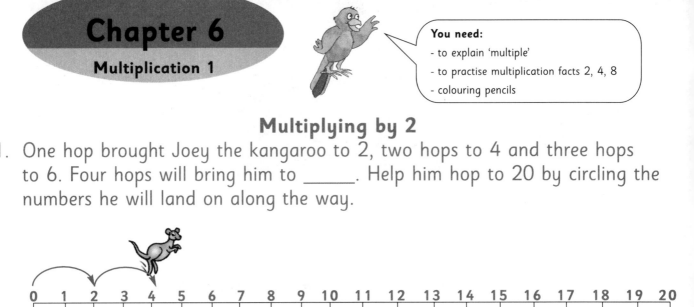

You need:
- to explain 'multiple'
- to practise multiplication facts 2, 4, 8
- colouring pencils

Multiplying by 2

1. One hop brought Joey the kangaroo to 2, two hops to 4 and three hops to 6. Four hops will bring him to _____. Help him hop to 20 by circling the numbers he will land on along the way.

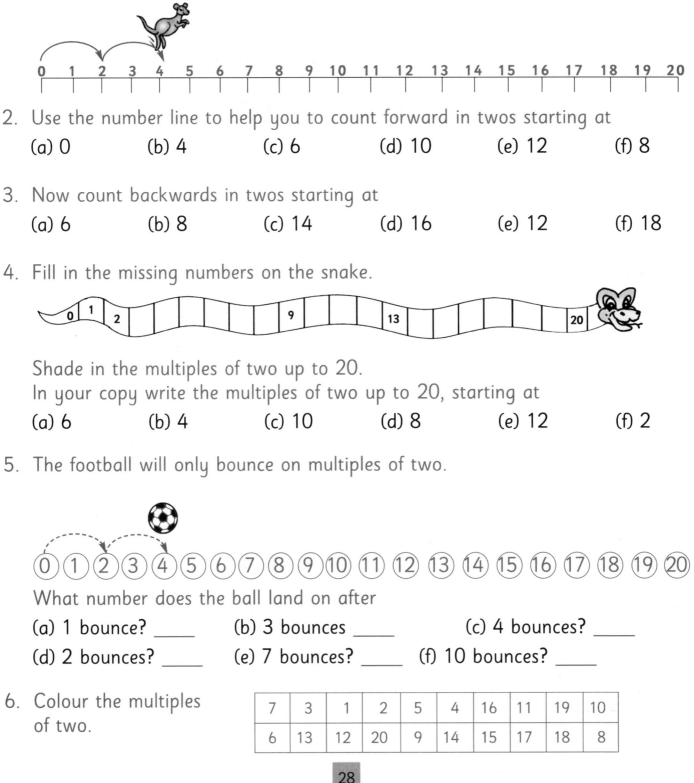

2. Use the number line to help you to count forward in twos starting at
   (a) 0   (b) 4   (c) 6   (d) 10   (e) 12   (f) 8

3. Now count backwards in twos starting at
   (a) 6   (b) 8   (c) 14   (d) 16   (e) 12   (f) 18

4. Fill in the missing numbers on the snake.

   Shade in the multiples of two up to 20.
   In your copy write the multiples of two up to 20, starting at
   (a) 6   (b) 4   (c) 10   (d) 8   (e) 12   (f) 2

5. The football will only bounce on multiples of two.

   What number does the ball land on after

   (a) 1 bounce? ____   (b) 3 bounces ____   (c) 4 bounces? ____
   (d) 2 bounces? ____   (e) 7 bounces? ____   (f) 10 bounces? ____

6. Colour the multiples of two.

7	3	1	2	5	4	16	11	19	10
6	13	12	20	9	14	15	17	18	8

Multiplication

$$\bigcirc\bigcirc + \bigcirc\bigcirc = 2 + 2 = 4 \quad \textbf{or} \quad 2 \times 2 = 4$$

$$\bigcirc\bigcirc + \bigcirc\bigcirc + \bigcirc\bigcirc = 2 + 2 + 2 = 6 \quad \textbf{or} \quad 3 \times 2 = 6$$

1. Write an addition sentence and a multiplication sentence for

   (a) $2 + 2 + 2 + 2 + 2 + 2 = $ _____ **or** _____ x 2 = _____

   (b) $2 + 2 + 2 + 2 + 2 + 2 + 2 = $ _____ **or** _____ x 2 = _____

   (c) $8 \times 2 = $ ___ **or** ___ + ___ + ___ + ___ + ___ + ___ + ___ + ___ = ___

   (d) $10 \times 2 = $ ___ **or** ___ + ___ + ___ + ___ + ___ + ___ + ___ + ___ + ___ + ___ = ___

2. In your copy write an addition sentence and a multiplication sentence for

   (a) Four twos   (b) Six twos   (c) Eight twos

   (d) Seven twos   (e) Ten twos   (f) Nine twos

3. Write the answers to these multiplication sentences.

   (a) $6 \times 2 = $ _____   (b) $3 \times 2 = $ _____   (c) $7 \times 2 = $ _____   (d) $5 \times 2 = $ _____

   (e) $8 \times 2 = $ _____   (f) $1 \times 2 = $ _____   (g) $10 \times 2 = $ _____   (h) $2 \times 2 = $ _____

4.

10	x 2	=	20
1	x 2	=	2
6	x 2	=	12
4	x 2	=	8
3	x 2	=	6
2	x 2	=	4
5	x 2	=	10
7	x 2	=	14
0	x 2	=	0
9	x 2	=	18
8	x 2	=	16

Put these multiplication sentences in the right order.

0	x 2	=
1	x 2	=

Multiplying by 2

1. How much money is in each moneybox?

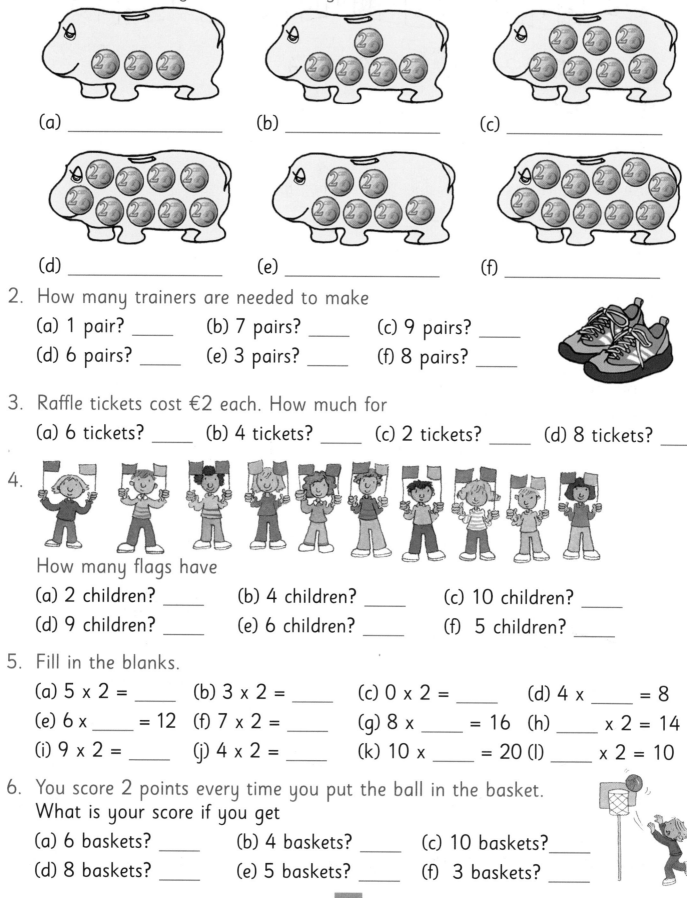

(a) _____   (b) _____   (c) _____

(d) _____   (e) _____   (f) _____

2. How many trainers are needed to make

(a) 1 pair? _____   (b) 7 pairs? _____   (c) 9 pairs? _____

(d) 6 pairs? _____   (e) 3 pairs? _____   (f) 8 pairs? _____

3. Raffle tickets cost €2 each. How much for

(a) 6 tickets? _____   (b) 4 tickets? _____   (c) 2 tickets? _____   (d) 8 tickets? _____

4.

How many flags have

(a) 2 children? _____   (b) 4 children? _____   (c) 10 children? _____

(d) 9 children? _____   (e) 6 children? _____   (f) 5 children? _____

5. Fill in the blanks.

(a) $5 \times 2 =$ _____   (b) $3 \times 2 =$ _____   (c) $0 \times 2 =$ _____   (d) $4 \times$ _____ $= 8$

(e) $6 \times$ _____ $= 12$ (f) $7 \times 2 =$ _____   (g) $8 \times$ _____ $= 16$ (h) _____ $\times 2 = 14$

(i) $9 \times 2 =$ _____   (j) $4 \times 2 =$ _____   (k) $10 \times$ _____ $= 20$ (l) _____ $\times 2 = 10$

6. You score 2 points every time you put the ball in the basket. What is your score if you get

(a) 6 baskets? _____   (b) 4 baskets? _____   (c) 10 baskets? _____

(d) 8 baskets? _____   (e) 5 baskets? _____   (f) 3 baskets? _____

Multiplying by 2

1. Write these sums both ways. The first one is done for you.

(a) Three twos $3 \times 2 = 6$ $\begin{array}{r} 2 \\ \times 3 \\ \hline 6 \end{array}$

(b) Five twos

(c) Seven twos

(d) Nine twos

(e) Eight twos

2. $\begin{array}{r} 2 \\ \times 6 \\ \hline \end{array}$ $\begin{array}{r} 2 \\ \times 7 \\ \hline \end{array}$ $\begin{array}{r} 2 \\ \times 10 \\ \hline \end{array}$ $\begin{array}{r} 2 \\ \times 1 \\ \hline \end{array}$ $\begin{array}{r} 2 \\ \times 4 \\ \hline \end{array}$ $\begin{array}{r} 2 \\ \times 9 \\ \hline \end{array}$ $\begin{array}{r} 2 \\ \times 2 \\ \hline \end{array}$ $\begin{array}{r} 2 \\ \times 8 \\ \hline \end{array}$

3. Write the answers to the sums in the grid below and then colour in the flower and the computer.

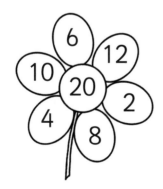

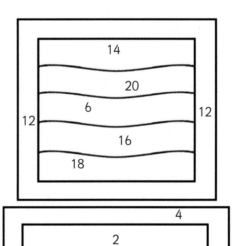

10 x 2	3 x 2	6 x 2	1 x 2	2 x 2	4 x 2	7 x 2	5 x 2	9 x 2	8 x 2
red	pink	blue	green	grey	yellow	white	brown	orange	black

Multiplying by 4

1. Joey is jumping in fours. Circle all his stopping places.

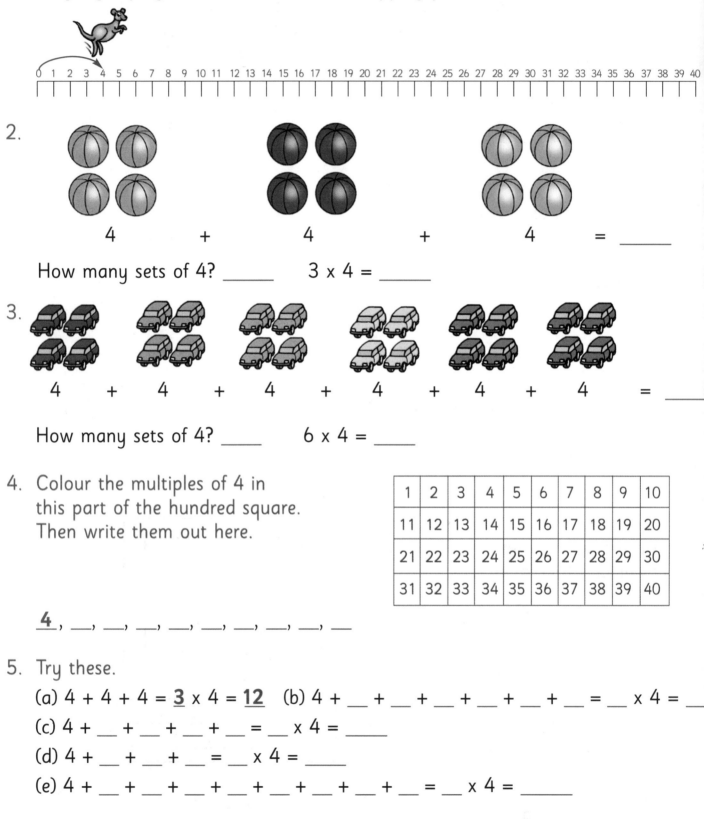

2.

4　　　　　+　　　　　4　　　　　+　　　　　4　　　　　=　_____

How many sets of 4? _____　　　3 x 4 = _____

3.

4　　+　　4　　+　　4　　+　　4　　+　　4　　+　　4　　　=　___

How many sets of 4? ____　　　6 x 4 = ____

4. Colour the multiples of 4 in this part of the hundred square. Then write them out here.

1	2	3	4	5	6	7	8	9	10
11	12	13	14	15	16	17	18	19	20
21	22	23	24	25	26	27	28	29	30
31	32	33	34	35	36	37	38	39	40

_4_, __, __, __, __, __, __, __, __, __

5. Try these.

(a) 4 + 4 + 4 = **3** x 4 = **12**　(b) 4 + __ + __ + __ + __ + __ + __ = __ x 4 = __

(c) 4 + __ + __ + __ + __ = __ x 4 = ____

(d) 4 + __ + __ + __ = __ x 4 = ____

(e) 4 + __ + __ + __ + __ + __ + __ + __ = __ x 4 = ____

6. Now try these.

(a) 7 x 4 = __　(b) 5 x 4 = __　(c) 10 x 4 = __　(d) 2 x 4 = __　(e) 8 x 4 = __

Multiplying by 4

1. Now try these.

   (a) 4   (b) 4   (c) 4   (d) 4   (e) 4
      x 5   x 9   x 6   x 2   x 4
      ____   ____   ____   ____   ____

   (f) 4   (g) 4   (h) 4   (i) 4   (j) 4
      x 3   x 1   x 7   x 10   x 8
      ____   ____   ____   ____   ____

2. How many legs have

    (a) 3 cows? _____   (b) 5 cows? _____   (c) 8 cows? _____

3. Ronan's Mammy buys 4 litres of milk every day.
   How many litres will she buy in a week? _____

4. One morning Jennifer saw 7 cars parked outside the
   school gate. She counted all the wheels of the cars.
   How many wheels did she count altogether? _____

5. Choose the numbers from the first barrel and multiply them by the number
   4 in the second barrel. Then find your answer in the third barrel.
   Colour the answers green. Did you find any 'uninvited guests'? _____
   Colour them red.

8 2 3
6 7 9
5 10
4

x 4

24 20
40 12 18
28 32 8
30 16 36

What did the numbers become?

(a) 3 x 4 = ___ (b) 2 x 4 = ___ (c) 8 x 4 = ___ (d) 6 x 4 = ___ (e) 7 x 4 = ___

(f) 9 x 4 = ___ (g) 5 x 4 = ___ (h) 10 x 4 = ___ (i) 4 x 4 = ___ (j) 1 x 4 = ___

Multiplying by 8

1. Joey is jumping in eights. Circle all his stopping places.

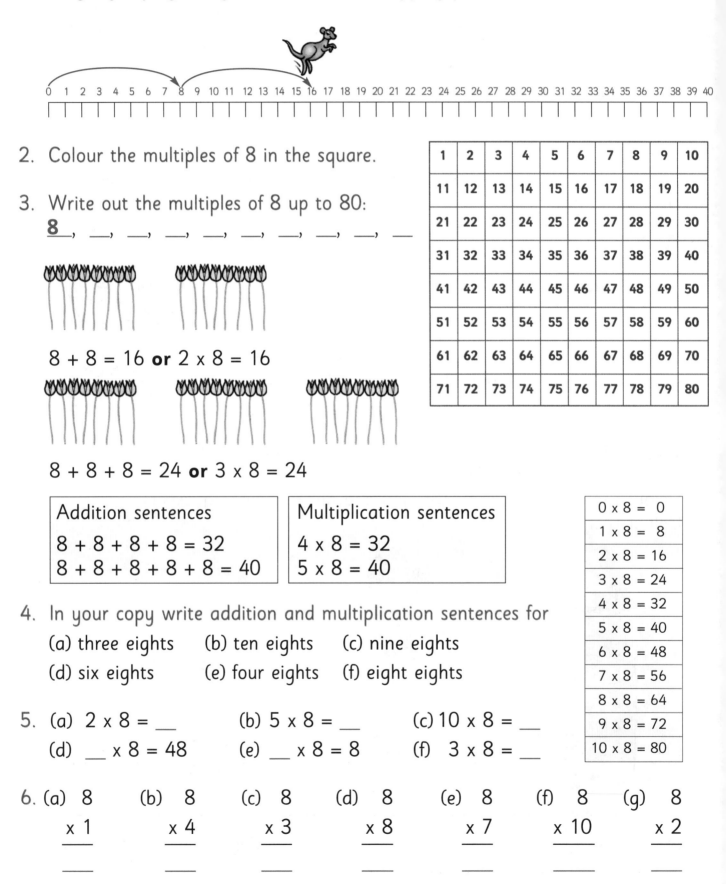

2. Colour the multiples of 8 in the square.

3. Write out the multiples of 8 up to 80:

   <u>8</u>, ___, ___, ___, ___, ___, ___, ___, ___, ___

8 + 8 = 16 **or** 2 x 8 = 16

8 + 8 + 8 = 24 **or** 3 x 8 = 24

1	2	3	4	5	6	7	8	9	10
11	12	13	14	15	16	17	18	19	20
21	22	23	24	25	26	27	28	29	30
31	32	33	34	35	36	37	38	39	40
41	42	43	44	45	46	47	48	49	50
51	52	53	54	55	56	57	58	59	60
61	62	63	64	65	66	67	68	69	70
71	72	73	74	75	76	77	78	79	80

Addition sentences	Multiplication sentences
8 + 8 + 8 + 8 = 32 8 + 8 + 8 + 8 + 8 = 40	4 x 8 = 32 5 x 8 = 40

0 x 8 = 0
1 x 8 = 8
2 x 8 = 16
3 x 8 = 24
4 x 8 = 32
5 x 8 = 40
6 x 8 = 48
7 x 8 = 56
8 x 8 = 64
9 x 8 = 72
10 x 8 = 80

4. In your copy write addition and multiplication sentences for
   (a) three eights   (b) ten eights   (c) nine eights
   (d) six eights   (e) four eights   (f) eight eights

5. (a) 2 x 8 = ___   (b) 5 x 8 = ___   (c) 10 x 8 = ___
   (d) ___ x 8 = 48   (e) ___ x 8 = 8   (f) 3 x 8 = ___

6. (a) 8   (b) 8   (c) 8   (d) 8   (e) 8   (f) 8   (g) 8
       x 1   x 4   x 3   x 8   x 7   x 10   x 2
      _____   _____   _____   _____   _____   _____   _____

      _____   _____   _____   _____   _____   _____   _____

Multiplying by 8

1. How many sweets in

          (a) 3 bags? ____   (b) 5 bags? ____   (c) 7 bags? ____

          (d) 4 bags? ____   (e) 6 bags? ____   (f) 9 bags? ____

2. How many pencils in

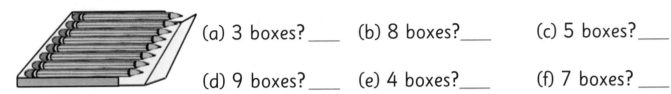

          (a) 3 boxes? ____   (b) 8 boxes?____   (c) 5 boxes?____

          (d) 9 boxes? ____   (e) 4 boxes?____   (f) 7 boxes? ____

3. How many children in

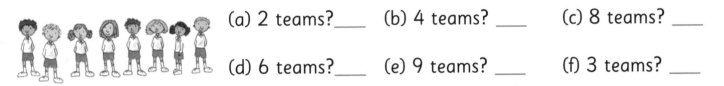

          (a) 2 teams?____   (b) 4 teams? ____   (c) 8 teams? ____

          (d) 6 teams?____   (e) 9 teams? ____   (f) 3 teams? ____

4. How much for

          (a) 2 lollipops? ____ (b) 4 lollipops? ____ (c) 8 lollipops? ____

          (d) 6 lollipops? ____ (e) 5 lollipops? ____ (f) 10 lollipops? ____

5. The teacher had 80 cards numbered 1 to 80. Each child in the class picked a card. The children who picked the multiples of eight won. Write the numbers they picked.

____, ____, ____, ____, ____, ____, ____, ____, ____, ____

6. Put this table in the right order.

10 x 8	0 x 8	6 x 8	9 x 8	1 x 8	3 x 8	5 x 8	7 x 8	2 x 8	4 x 8	8 x 8
72	48	8	16	80	64	32	0	56	24	40

0 x 8										
0										

You need:
- lollipop sticks or counters
- colouring pencils
- to practise 2, 4 and 8 division facts

Sharing between 2

1. Share these sweets equally between Ciara and Conor.
   Draw the sweets in their party bags and then colour them.

How many sweets did each child get? _____

8 sweets divided equally between 2 children is 4 sweets each.
In Mathematics this sentence can be written as a division sentence
like this: **8 ÷ 2 = 4.** The symbol ÷ means 'shared' or 'divided'.

2. Fiona and her brother James sat at the kitchen table and shared this packet
   of animal stickers equally between them. Draw and colour the number of
   stickers that each child got on the table in front of them.

Write a division sentence to show how they shared the stickers.
This should help you: 12 ÷ 2 = _____

Sharing among 2 and 4

1. Mammy baked 16 chocolate buns for tea and shared them equally among her four children, Adam, Barbara, Brian and Aisling.
Draw and colour the number of cakes on each of the children's plates.

How many buns did each child get? ____
16 buns divided equally among 4 children is 4 buns each.
Now write a division sentence to show how they shared the buns.
This should help you: 16 ÷ 4 = ____

2. Share 16 counters or lollipop sticks equally

   (a) between your friend and yourself. Each of you gets ____

   (b) among three other friends and yourself. Each of you gets ____

   Now share 20 counters or lollipop sticks in the same way.
   When you have finished, fill in the missing numbers below.

   (a) 16 ÷ 2 = ____   (b) 16 ÷ 4 = ____   (c) 20 ÷ ____ = 10   (d) 20 ÷ 4 = ____

3. Use counters or lollipop sticks to do these.

   (a) 8 ÷ 2 = ___   (b) 18 ÷ 2 = ___   (c) 10 ÷ 2 = ___   (d) 4 ÷ 2 = ___

   (e) 12 ÷ 2 = ___   (f) 6 ÷ 2 = ___   (g) 2 ÷ 2 = ___   (h) 14 ÷ 2 = ___

4. Now try these.

   (a) 8 ÷ 4 = ___   (b) 12 ÷ 4 = ___   (c) 24 ÷ 4 = ___   (d) 20 ÷ 4 = ___

   (e) 4 ÷ 4 = ___   (f) 40 ÷ 4 = ___   (g) 32 ÷ 4 = ___   (h) 28 ÷ 4 = ___

Sharing among 8

1. After Ronan's birthday party he shared a multi-pack of crisps among his 8 friends to bring home with them.
How many packs did each child bring home? ____
16 packs divided among 8 children is 2 packs for each child.
You can write this as a division sentence like this: 16 ÷ 8 = 2

2. Share 40 lollipop sticks equally among 8 children in your class.
How many did each child get? ____
Write what you did with the lollipop sticks as a division sentence.

__ ÷ __ = __

3. Write these stories as division sentences.
(a) 24 marbles divided among 8 boys is 3 marbles each.

__ ÷ __ = __

(b) A prize of €40 shared among 8 winners is €5 each.

__ ÷ __ = __

(c) 80 counters divided equally among 8 children is 10 counters each.

__ ÷ __ = __

4. Try these.
(a) 8 ÷ 8 = ____ (b) 48 ÷ 8 = ____ (c) 32 ÷ 8 = ____ (d) 40 ÷ 8 = ____
(e) 64 ÷ 8 = ____ (f) 56 ÷ 8 = ____ (g) 72 ÷ 8 = ____ (h) 80 ÷ 8 = ____

5. Share these marbles among the children in the picture.

(a) How many marbles are there? ____
(b) How many children? ____
(c) How many marbles does each child get? ____
(d) Write this story as a division sentence. ____ ÷ ____ = ____

6.

The zookeeper shared 56 bananas among the 8 monkeys. How many bananas did each monkey get? ____

Division as groups

1. Look at these 20 cent coins.
   (a) There are _____ coins altogether.
   (b) Divide them into groups of 2 with
       your pencil. The first group is done
       for you. There are _____ groups of 2.
   You can write this as a division sentence like this: 6 ÷ 2 = 3.

2. Take 14 counters or lollipop sticks and divide them into groups of 2.
   (a) How many groups of 2 did you get? _____
   (b) Write it as a division sentence like this: _____ ÷ 2 = _____

3. How many groups of
   (a) 2 apples in a box of 8 apples? _____
   (b) 2 oranges in a box of 12 oranges? _____

4. How many teams of 2 can be made from 16 pupils? _____

5. How many sets of 2 lollipop sticks can be made out of 18? _____

6. How many 2c coins make up a 20c coin? _____

7. There are 32 children in Ms Kelly's class.
   She brought them on a nature walk
   and divided them into groups of 4.
   (a) How many groups were there? _____
   (b) Write it as a division sentence _____ ÷ _____ = _____

8. With your partner get 24 counters or lollipop sticks and divide them
   into groups of 4.
   (a) How many groups did you get? _____
   (b) Write it as a division sentence _____ ÷ _____ = _____

9. How many 4's in
   (a) 12 _____   (b) 16 _____   (c) 20 _____   (d) 28 _____   (e) 16 _____   (f) 40 _____

10. 48 children took part in a hike organised by the Ballybeg Youth Club.
    The leaders divided them into groups of 8. How many groups were there
    altogether? _____ Write it as a division sentence _____ ÷ _____ = _____

Division as groups

1. Divide these cards into groups of 8 with your pencil. The first group is done for you.
   (a) How many cards are there? _____
   (b) How many in each group? _____
   (c) How many groups are there? _____
   (d) Write it as a division sentence _____ ÷ _____ = _____

2. Divide these apples into groups of 8.
   (a) How many apples are there? _____
   (b) How many in each group? _____
   (c) How many groups are there? _____
   (d) Write it as a division sentence ___ ÷ ___ = ___

3. Use counters or lollipop sticks to do the following questions.
   (a) 16 ÷ 2 = _____   (b) 20 ÷ 2 = _____   (c) 28 ÷ 4 = _____   (d) 32 ÷ 4 = _____
   (e) 40 ÷ 4 = _____   (f) 40 ÷ 8 = _____   (g) 56 ÷ 8 = _____   (h) 72 ÷ 8 = _____

4. Markers are sold in packets of 4. How many packets are needed for 28 markers? _____

5.  A minibus can hold 8 children. How many minibuses are needed to bring 24 children to a match? _____

6. The O'Briens sell some of their apples to the local supermarket. Yesterday they picked 36 apples and packed them in bags of 4.

   How many bags did they need? _____

   Write it as a division sentence _____ ÷ _____ = _____

7.  In Glenmore Primary School the third classes have 32 girls and 24 boys. How many groups can be made from the two classes if there are 8 children in each group? _____

   Write it as a division sentence. _____ ÷ _____ = _____

Dividing by 2, 4 and 8

Match the correct numbers in each set. The first one is done for you.

÷ 2		÷ 4		÷ 8	
10	8	32	6	56	7
20	10	24	10	80	5
16	5	40	8	40	10

In what year did Vesuvius erupt?

Vesuvius is a volcanic mountain in Italy. Many years ago it erupted and the nearby town of Pompeii disappeared under the ash. It was forgotten about for nearly 1700 years until excavators dug down and uncovered most of the town and about 2000 people frozen in time.

To find the year that Vesuvius erupted, cross out all the numbers in the box that can be divided into groups of 2, 4 or 8. One number has already been crossed out for you. (12 may be crossed out because it can be divided into groups of 2 **or** groups of 4.)

$12 \div 2 = 6$
$12 \div 4 = 3$

17	20	80
16	24	64
48	43	12
18	36	10
19	56	32

When you have finished, add up the three numbers that are left. The answer you get will tell you the year that Vesuvius erupted.

Answer: _____ + _____ + _____ = _____ AD

You need:
- to explain 'fraction' as 'part of'
- to demonstrate folding
- colouring pencils

1. You need 3 paper rectangles, 20cm long and 4cm wide.
   (a) Write 1 unit on the first rectangle like this:

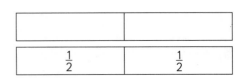

   (b) Fold the second rectangle in half to make 2
      equal parts like this:
      Each part is called a half.
      Write in the halves like this:

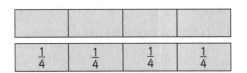

   (c) Fold the third rectangle in half and in
      half again like this:
      Each part is called a quarter.
      Write in the quarters like this:

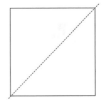

   (d) Pick a colour for each rectangle and put
      your fraction wall on your table like this:

2.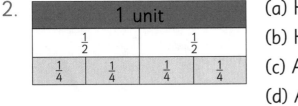

   (a) How many halves in one unit? _____
   (b) How many quarters in one unit? _____
   (c) Are the two halves the same size? _____
   (d) Are the four quarters the same size? _____
   (e) How many quarters in a half? _____

3. Two of these shapes have been divided into halves. Find and colour them.

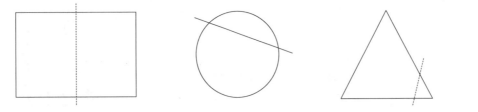

4. Two of these shapes have been divided into quarters. Find and colour them.

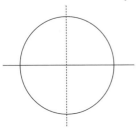 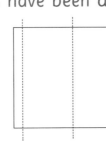 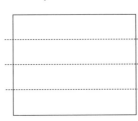 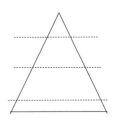

Halves and quarters

1.

1 unit				1 unit				1 unit			
$\frac{1}{2}$		$\frac{1}{2}$		$\frac{1}{2}$		$\frac{1}{2}$		$\frac{1}{2}$		$\frac{1}{2}$	
$\frac{1}{4}$	$\frac{1}{4}$	$\frac{1}{4}$	$\frac{1}{4}$	$\frac{1}{4}$	$\frac{1}{4}$	$\frac{1}{4}$	$\frac{1}{4}$	$\frac{1}{4}$	$\frac{1}{4}$	$\frac{1}{4}$	$\frac{1}{4}$

(a) Write in 1 unit, two halves and four quarters.

(b) Colour $\frac{1}{2}$. Colour the first two quarters.

(c) Colour $\frac{3}{4}$.

2. Which is bigger?

(a) $\frac{1}{2}$ or $\frac{1}{4}$ ☐

(b) $\frac{1}{2}$ or $\frac{3}{4}$ ☐

(c) 1 or $\boxed{2}$

(d) 1 or $\boxed{4}$

3.

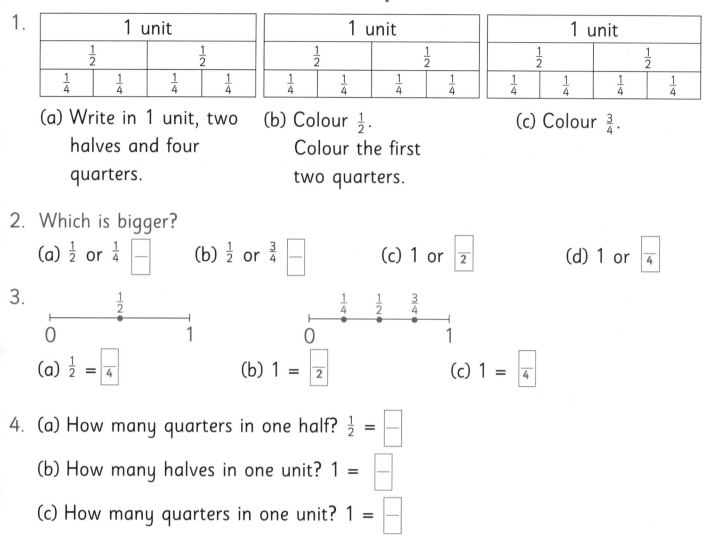

(a) $\frac{1}{2} = \boxed{\dfrac{}{4}}$

(b) $1 = \boxed{\dfrac{}{2}}$

(c) $1 = \boxed{\dfrac{}{4}}$

4. (a) How many quarters in one half? $\frac{1}{2} = \boxed{\dfrac{}{}}$

(b) How many halves in one unit? $1 = \boxed{\dfrac{}{}}$

(c) How many quarters in one unit? $1 = \boxed{\dfrac{}{}}$

5. Look at these pictures. They will help you to fill in the missing numbers on this number line.

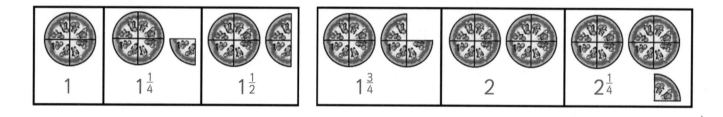

| 1 | $1\frac{1}{4}$ | $1\frac{1}{2}$ | $1\frac{3}{4}$ | 2 | $2\frac{1}{4}$ | |

0 $\frac{1}{4}$ $\frac{1}{2}$ $\frac{3}{4}$ 1 $1\frac{1}{4}$ 2 $2\frac{3}{4}$ 4

Eighths

1. You now need a fourth rectangle.
Fold the rectangle so that it is divided
into 8 equal parts like this:

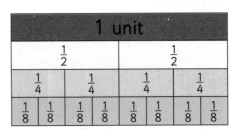

   Are all the parts the same size? _____
Each part is called **one eighth or** $\frac{1}{8}$.
Write $\frac{1}{8}$ in each part of your
rectangle and colour it.

   Now put your fraction wall
on your table like this:

1 unit							
$\frac{1}{2}$				$\frac{1}{2}$			
$\frac{1}{4}$		$\frac{1}{4}$		$\frac{1}{4}$		$\frac{1}{4}$	
$\frac{1}{8}$	$\frac{1}{8}$	$\frac{1}{8}$	$\frac{1}{8}$	$\frac{1}{8}$	$\frac{1}{8}$	$\frac{1}{8}$	$\frac{1}{8}$

2. Find and colour the shapes that are divided into eight **equal** parts.

   (a) 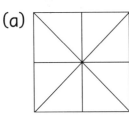   (b) 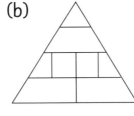   (c) 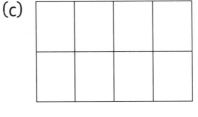   (d)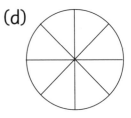

3. What fraction of these rectangles is coloured?

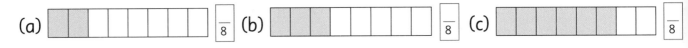

   (a) $\frac{}{8}$ (b) $\frac{}{8}$ (c) $\frac{}{8}$

4. Colour the fractions shown.

   (a) $\frac{5}{8}$ (b) $\frac{7}{8}$ (c) $\frac{8}{8}$

5.

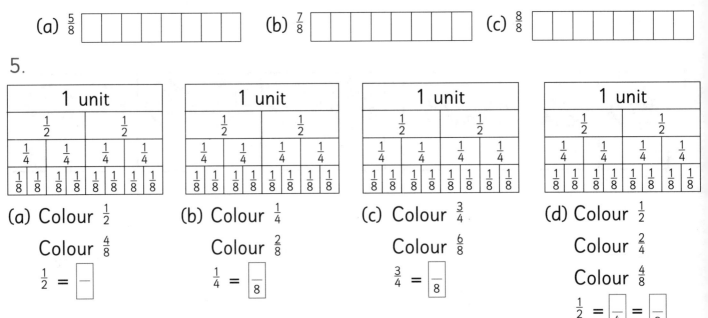

   (a) Colour $\frac{1}{2}$

       Colour $\frac{4}{8}$

       $\frac{1}{2} = \frac{}{}$

   (b) Colour $\frac{1}{4}$

       Colour $\frac{2}{8}$

       $\frac{1}{4} = \frac{}{8}$

   (c) Colour $\frac{3}{4}$

       Colour $\frac{6}{8}$

       $\frac{3}{4} = \frac{}{8}$

   (d) Colour $\frac{1}{2}$

       Colour $\frac{2}{4}$

       Colour $\frac{4}{8}$

       $\frac{1}{2} = \frac{}{4} = \frac{}{8}$

Halves, quarters and eighths

1. Do these and use your answers to fill in the missing fractions on the number line. Use your fraction wall to help you.

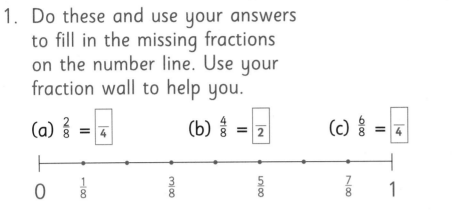

(a) $\frac{2}{8} = \frac{\square}{4}$ (b) $\frac{4}{8} = \frac{\square}{2}$ (c) $\frac{6}{8} = \frac{\square}{4}$

```
|----•----•----•----•----•----•----•----|
0    1/8       3/8       5/8       7/8      1
```

2. Use these pictures to help you fill in the blanks on the number line below.

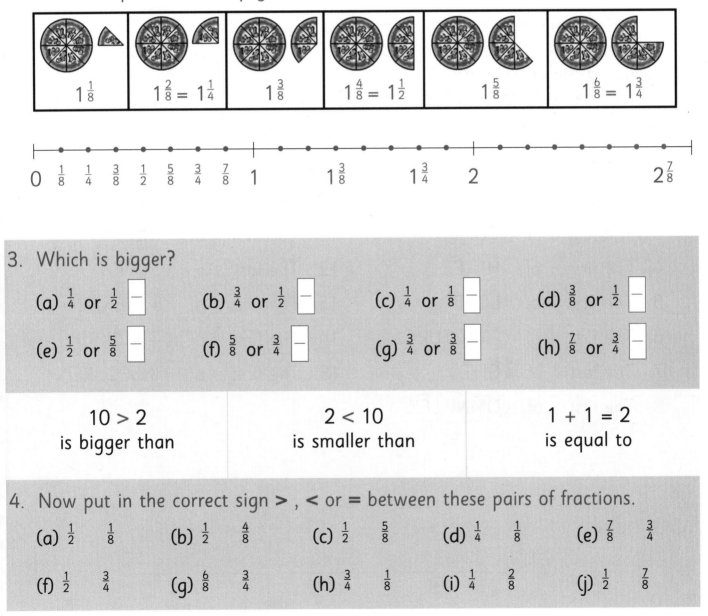

$1\frac{1}{8}$ $1\frac{2}{8} = 1\frac{1}{4}$ $1\frac{3}{8}$ $1\frac{4}{8} = 1\frac{1}{2}$ $1\frac{5}{8}$ $1\frac{6}{8} = 1\frac{3}{4}$

```
|--•--•--•--•--•--•--•--|--•--•--•--•--•--•--•--|--•--•--•--•--•--•--•--|
0  1/8 1/4 3/8 1/2 5/8 3/4 7/8  1        1 3/8      1 3/4     2                    2 7/8
```

3. Which is bigger?

(a) $\frac{1}{4}$ or $\frac{1}{2}$ ☐ (b) $\frac{3}{4}$ or $\frac{1}{2}$ ☐ (c) $\frac{1}{4}$ or $\frac{1}{8}$ ☐ (d) $\frac{3}{8}$ or $\frac{1}{2}$ ☐

(e) $\frac{1}{2}$ or $\frac{5}{8}$ ☐ (f) $\frac{5}{8}$ or $\frac{3}{4}$ ☐ (g) $\frac{3}{4}$ or $\frac{3}{8}$ ☐ (h) $\frac{7}{8}$ or $\frac{3}{4}$ ☐

10 > 2	2 < 10	1 + 1 = 2
is bigger than	is smaller than	is equal to

4. Now put in the correct sign **>** , **<** or **=** between these pairs of fractions.

(a) $\frac{1}{2}$ $\frac{1}{8}$ (b) $\frac{1}{2}$ $\frac{4}{8}$ (c) $\frac{1}{2}$ $\frac{5}{8}$ (d) $\frac{1}{4}$ $\frac{1}{8}$ (e) $\frac{7}{8}$ $\frac{3}{4}$

(f) $\frac{1}{2}$ $\frac{3}{4}$ (g) $\frac{6}{8}$ $\frac{3}{4}$ (h) $\frac{3}{4}$ $\frac{1}{8}$ (i) $\frac{1}{4}$ $\frac{2}{8}$ (j) $\frac{1}{2}$ $\frac{7}{8}$

The train is coming

A tourist came to a level crossing with one gate open and the other shut. He said to the boy standing nearby, 'Why is one gate open and the other shut?'
To find the boy's answer, find the fraction of each word below. Then write the letters, in order, into the boxes at the bottom of the page.

1. The first $\frac{1}{2}$ of WENT
2. The last $\frac{1}{2}$ of STAR
3. The last $\frac{1}{4}$ of BONE
4. The first $\frac{1}{2}$ of HATE
5. The first $\frac{1}{4}$ of LOVE
6. The first $\frac{1}{8}$ of FRACTURE
7. The last $\frac{1}{4}$ of GIVE
8. The last $\frac{1}{8}$ of OMNIPLEX

9. The last $\frac{1}{2}$ of ROPE
10. The first $\frac{1}{4}$ of CROW
11. The first $\frac{1}{2}$ of TIDE
12. The last $\frac{1}{2}$ of SONG
13. The first $\frac{1}{8}$ of ATTENDED
14. The first $\frac{1}{2}$ of TRACKS
15. The first $\frac{1}{4}$ of INSECURE

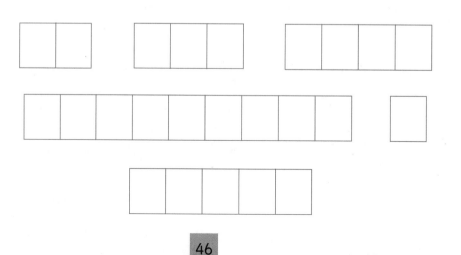

46

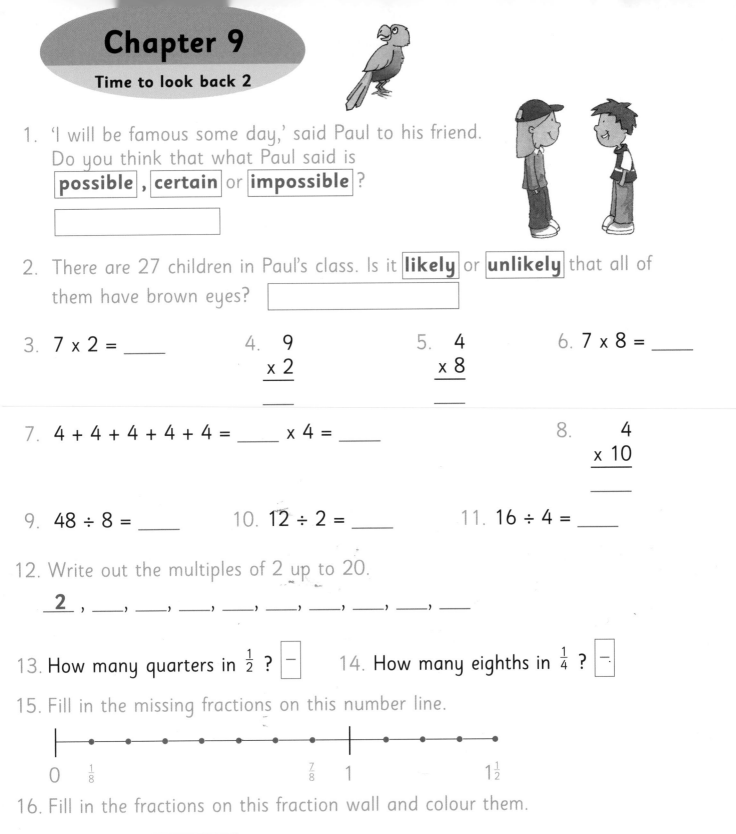

1. 'I will be famous some day,' said Paul to his friend. Do you think that what Paul said is possible , certain or impossible ?

2. There are 27 children in Paul's class. Is it likely or unlikely that all of them have brown eyes?

3. $7 \times 2 = $ ____

4. $\begin{array}{r} 9 \\ \times 2 \\ \hline \end{array}$

5. $\begin{array}{r} 4 \\ \times 8 \\ \hline \end{array}$

6. $7 \times 8 = $ ____

7. $4 + 4 + 4 + 4 + 4 = $ ____ $\times 4 = $ ____

8. $\begin{array}{r} 4 \\ \times 10 \\ \hline \end{array}$

9. $48 \div 8 = $ ____

10. $12 \div 2 = $ ____

11. $16 \div 4 = $ ____

12. Write out the multiples of 2 up to 20.

   __2__ , ____, ____, ____, ____, ____, ____, ____, ____, ____

13. How many quarters in $\frac{1}{2}$? ☐

14. How many eighths in $\frac{1}{4}$? ☐

15. Fill in the missing fractions on this number line.

   0    $\frac{1}{8}$ $\frac{7}{8}$ 1 $1\frac{1}{2}$

16. Fill in the fractions on this fraction wall and colour them.

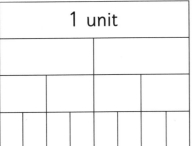

47

17. Paul's class was brought to the local swimming pool. The pool was divided into 5 lanes. The instructor put 4 children in each lane. **How many children were in the pool?** _____

18. Eight of the children needed 2 armbands each. **How many armbands were needed altogether?** _____

19. After the swim, Paul's friend Pat bought 2 bars. He gave $\frac{1}{2}$ a bar to each of his 3 friends. **What fraction of a bar had he left for himself?** [—]

20. Four of the children shared 40c equally. **How much did each child get?** _____

How well did you do?

Give yourself 1 mark for each question you answered correctly and then tick the box with your score.

☐	☐	☐	☐
18–20 Excellent	15–17 Very good	10–14 Good	0–9 Keep up the good work

You need:
- to revise angles
- lollipop sticks or geostrips
- cardboard or plastic 2-D shapes

1. (a) Name each shape.

square
triangle
- rectangle

_____   _____   _____

(b) Colour all the angles in red.
(c) In the grid write the number of
    sides and the number of angles
    for each shape.

	Number of sides	Number of angles
Square		
Triangle		
Rectangle		

2. Name each shape.

(a)   (b)   (c)

semi-circle
oval
circle

_____   _____   _____

One shape has a curved **and** a straight side. Which one? _____

3. Make
   (a) a square using 4 geostrips   (b) a rectangle using 4 geostrips
   (c) a triangle using 3 geostrips

4. Make
   (a) a square using 8 geostrips
   (b) a rectangle using 12 geostrips
   (c) a triangle using 6 geostrips

5. See how many different shapes you can make with
   (a) 6 geostrips   (b) 12 geostrips

6. Two of these triangles put together will make a _____

   Two squares will make a _____

   Two semi-circles will make a _____

Hexagon

1. Hexagon is a Greek word that means 'six-sided'. Colour the shapes in the box below that are hexagons.

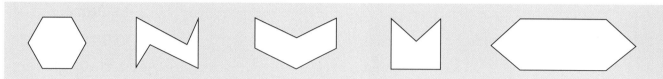

   How many of the hexagons have 6 equal sides? _____

2. This is a regular hexagon. It has 6 equal sides and 6 equal angles.

   (a) how many sides? _____
   (b) how many angles? _____

3. Make
   (a) a regular hexagon using 6 geostrips
   (b) a regular hexagon using 12 geostrips

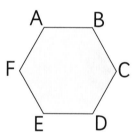

4. In your copy draw around a regular hexagon and then mark the corners with the letters A, B, C, D, E and F like this:

   Now use your ruler and pencil and draw straight lines from corner to corner, from (a) A to C (b) C to E (c) E to A (d) B to D (e) D to F (f) F to B
   What shapes have you made? _____ Colour the shapes in the hexagon.

5.   Six of these triangles will make a _____

6. Look around and see if you can see six things that are shaped like these.

   Now draw the things you spotted.

Tessellation

When shapes fit together without leaving a space between them we say that they **tessellate.**

1. Put an x beside the shapes do not tessellate?

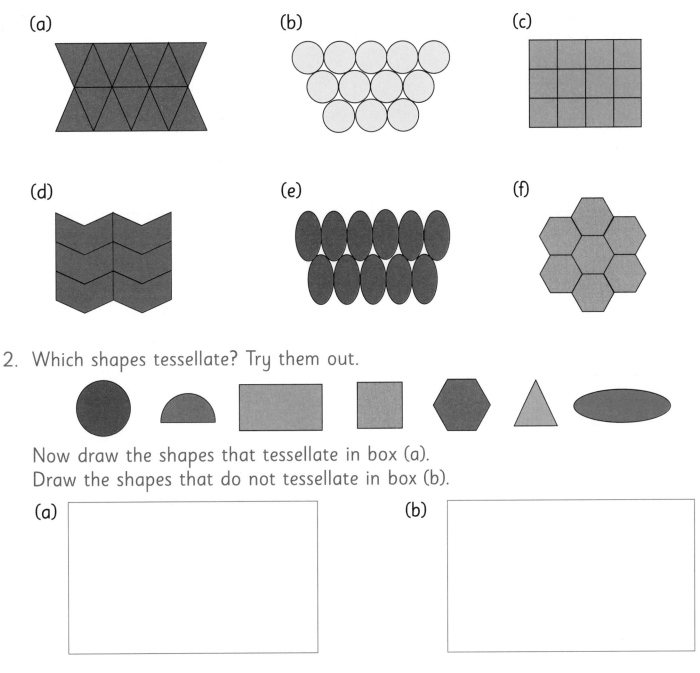

(a)

(b)

(c)

(d)

(e)

(f)

2. Which shapes tessellate? Try them out.

Now draw the shapes that tessellate in box (a).
Draw the shapes that do not tessellate in box (b).

(a)

(b)

What did you discover about the curved shapes? _____

_____

3. Design and colour your own tessellation for display. Use squared paper or trace around shapes if you wish.

Have fun with shapes

You are going to draw a picture of a house and garden in the rectangle below. You must follow these instructions very carefully!

1. Begin with the dotted square in the middle.

    (a) Put a triangle on top of the square. This is your roof.

    (b) Put two rectangular windows upstairs.

    (c) Draw the rectangular front door in the middle of the house.

    (d) Put a glass panel shaped like a hexagon in the front door.

    (e) You need a square window on either side of the front door.

    (f) Draw a rectangular chimney on the right hand side of the roof.

    (g) Lastly, put two circular flower beds in the front garden.

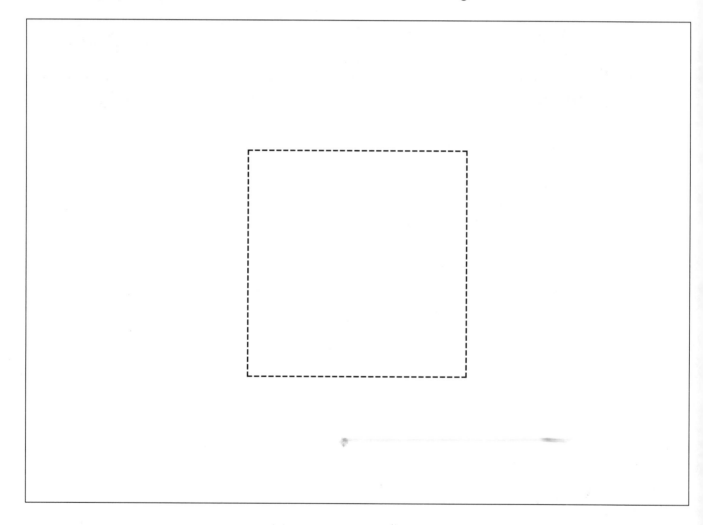

2. Compare your picture with the pictures that other children in your group drew.

3. Finish the picture using other shapes if you can. Colour your work.

Chapter 11
Multiplication 2

You need:
- to explain multiple
- to practise multiplication facts 3, 6, 9
- colouring pencils

Multiplying by 3

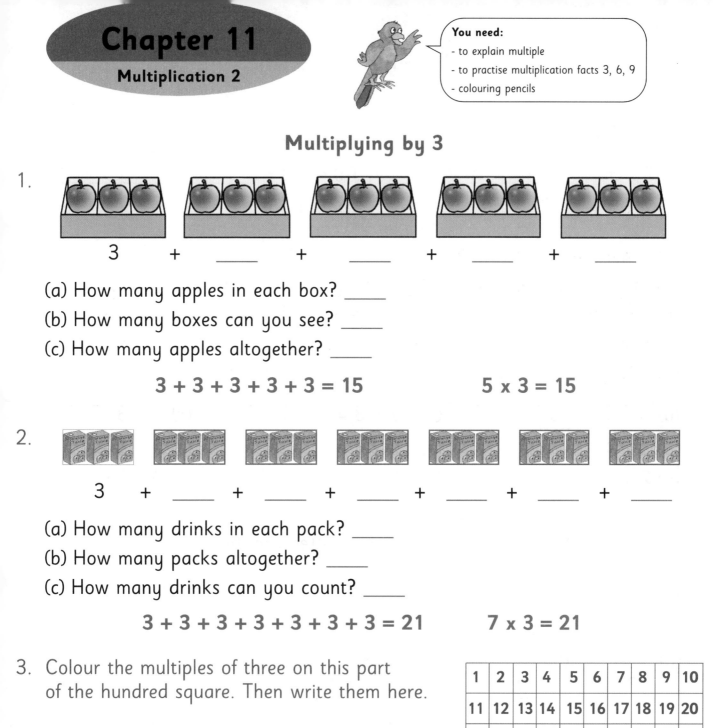

1.

3 + _____ + _____ + _____ + _____

(a) How many apples in each box? _____

(b) How many boxes can you see? _____

(c) How many apples altogether? _____

3 + 3 + 3 + 3 + 3 = 15   5 x 3 = 15

2.

3 + _____ + _____ + _____ + _____ + _____ + _____

(a) How many drinks in each pack? _____

(b) How many packs altogether? _____

(c) How many drinks can you count? _____

3 + 3 + 3 + 3 + 3 + 3 + 3 = 21   7 x 3 = 21

3. Colour the multiples of three on this part of the hundred square. Then write them here.

1	2	3	4	5	6	7	8	9	10
11	12	13	14	15	16	17	18	19	20
21	22	23	24	25	26	27	28	29	30

____ , ____ , ____ , ____ , ____ , ____ , ____ , ____ , ____ , ____

Use these multiples of three to count forwards and backwards in threes.

4. In your copy write a multiplication sentence for these addition sentences.
   (a) 3 + 3 = 6   (b) 3 + 3 + 3 + 3 + 3 = 15   (c) 3 + 3 + 3 + 3 = 12
   (d) 3 + 3 + 3 + 3 + 3 + 3 + 3 + 3 = 24   (e) 3 + 3 + 3 + 3 + 3 + 3 = 18

Multiplying by 3

1. Try these.

   (a) 3 x 3 = **3 + 3 + 3** _____   (b) 8 x 3 = _____

   (c) 5 x 3 = _____   (d) 4 x 3 = _____

   (e) 7 x 3 = _____   (f) 9 x 3 = _____

2. How many buns in

   (a) 6 packs? _____   (b) 4 packs? _____   (c) 5 packs? _____

   (d) 9 packs? _____   (e) 3 packs? _____   (f) 8 packs? _____

3. Now try these.

   (a) 5 x 3 = __15__   (b) 7 x 3 = ____   (c) 9 x 3 = ____

   (d) 3 x 3 = ____   (e) 8 x 3 = ____   (f) 6 x 3 = ____

   (g) 2 x 3 = ____   (h) 10 x 3 = ____   (i) 4 x 3 = ____

   (8 x 3 = 24)   can also be written like this
   $$\begin{array}{r} 3 \\ \times\, 8 \\ \hline 24 \end{array}$$

4. Try these.

   (a) $\begin{array}{r} 3 \\ \times\, 3 \\ \hline \end{array}$
   (b) $\begin{array}{r} 3 \\ \times\, 9 \\ \hline \end{array}$
   (c) $\begin{array}{r} 3 \\ \times\, 5 \\ \hline \end{array}$
   (d) $\begin{array}{r} 3 \\ \times\, 10 \\ \hline \end{array}$
   (e) $\begin{array}{r} 3 \\ \times\, 4 \\ \hline \end{array}$
   (f) $\begin{array}{r} 3 \\ \times\, 6 \\ \hline \end{array}$

5. Niamh's Dad spends €3 on train fares to work every day. He does not work on Saturdays or Sundays. How much does it cost him to travel to work for a week? _____

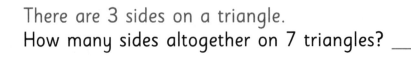

6. There are 3 sides on a triangle. How many sides altogether on 7 triangles? _____

54

Party time

1. It was Aisling's ninth birthday last week. The postman delivered 3 birthday cards on Monday, 3 more on Tuesday and another 3 on Wednesday. How many cards did he deliver over the 3 days? _____

2. Aisling's mother brought Aisling and nine of her friends to the cinema on her birthday. The cinema tickets cost €3 each. How much did Aisling's mother pay altogether for Aisling and her friends? _____

3. When Aisling and her friends came back to the house after the cinema, Aisling's mother gave each of them a chocolate ice-cream. The ice-creams were in packs of three. Aisling's mother had bought 4 packs. How many ice-creams did she buy? _____

The Gentle Giant

The giant cannot find the path to his castle. He has to follow the path marked with multiples of 3 to reach his castle safely. Help him to find the correct path by colouring all the multiples of three and the paths between them.

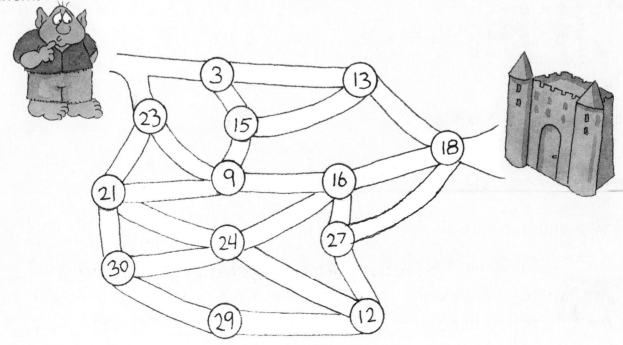

Multiplying by 6

1.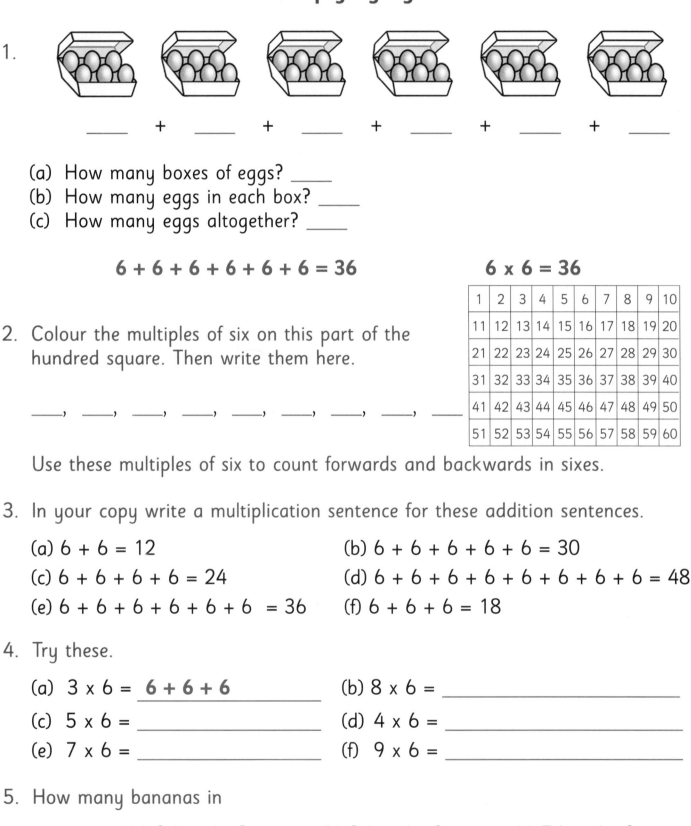

   _____ + _____ + _____ + _____ + _____ + _____

   (a) How many boxes of eggs? _____
   (b) How many eggs in each box? _____
   (c) How many eggs altogether? _____

   6 + 6 + 6 + 6 + 6 + 6 = 36   **6 x 6 = 36**

2. Colour the multiples of six on this part of the hundred square. Then write them here.

1	2	3	4	5	6	7	8	9	10
11	12	13	14	15	16	17	18	19	20
21	22	23	24	25	26	27	28	29	30
31	32	33	34	35	36	37	38	39	40
41	42	43	44	45	46	47	48	49	50
51	52	53	54	55	56	57	58	59	60

   ____, ____, ____, ____, ____, ____, ____, ____, ____

   Use these multiples of six to count forwards and backwards in sixes.

3. In your copy write a multiplication sentence for these addition sentences.

   (a) 6 + 6 = 12   (b) 6 + 6 + 6 + 6 + 6 = 30
   (c) 6 + 6 + 6 + 6 = 24   (d) 6 + 6 + 6 + 6 + 6 + 6 + 6 + 6 = 48
   (e) 6 + 6 + 6 + 6 + 6 + 6 = 36   (f) 6 + 6 + 6 = 18

4. Try these.

   (a) 3 x 6 = **6 + 6 + 6**_____   (b) 8 x 6 = _____
   (c) 5 x 6 = _____   (d) 4 x 6 = _____
   (e) 7 x 6 = _____   (f) 9 x 6 = _____

5. How many bananas in

   (a) 2 bunches? _____   (b) 3 bunches? _____   (c) 7 bunches? _____
   (d) 9 bunches? _____   (e) 4 bunches? _____   (f) 8 bunches? _____
   (g) 10 bunches? _____   (h) 5 bunches? _____   (i) 6 bunches? _____

Multiplying by 6 again

$8 \times 6 = 48$ can also be written like this

$$\begin{array}{r} 8 \\ \times\ 6 \\ \hline 48 \end{array}$$

1. Try these.

(a) 6
   x 3
   ___

(b) 6
   x 9
   ___

(c) 6
   x 5
   ___

(d) 6
   x 10
   ___

(e) 6
   x 4
   ___

(f) 6
   x 6
   ___

2. A hexagon is a shape with 6 sides.
   How many sides altogether have 5 hexagons? ____

3.  There are 6 apples on each tray.
   How many apples are there on:
   (a) 7 trays? ____   (b) 9 trays? ____

4. The milkman delivers 8 litres of milk to Niamh's
   house every day and none on Sundays. **How many
   litres does he deliver to the house in a week?** ____

5. A wasp has 6 legs. How many legs altogether have 4 wasps? _____

Top Secret

In the boxes below cross out the numbers that are **not multiples of 6**
and the letters underneath those numbers. Look carefully under the
numbers that are left and you will find a very important message.
Keep it a secret.

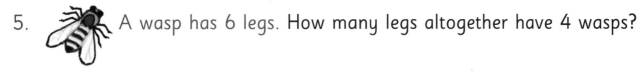

18	16	56	30	24	46	48	28	36	14	54	42	50	60	6	12
I	S	P	A	M	O	T	R	H	N	E	B	U	E	S	T

Multiplying by 9

1. Write the number of rungs under each ladder.

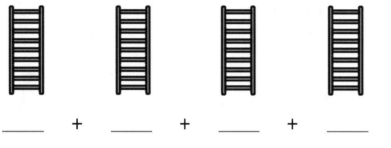

___ + ___ + ___ + ___ + ___ + ___

9 + 9 + 9 + 9 + 9 + 9 = 54　　　　　　**6 x 9 = 54**

2. Count in nines on this part of the 100 square. Colour the multiples of 9. In your copy write addition and multiplication sentences for these.

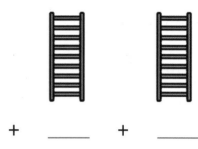

1	2	3	4	5	6	7	8	9	10
11	12	13	14	15	16	17	18	19	20
21	22	23	24	25	26	27	28	29	30
31	32	33	34	35	36	37	38	39	40
41	42	43	44	45	46	47	48	49	50
51	52	53	54	55	56	57	58	59	60
61	62	63	64	65	66	67	68	69	70
71	72	73	74	75	76	77	78	79	80
81	82	83	84	85	86	87	88	89	90

(a) 27　　**9 + 9 + 9 = 27**　　**3 x 9 = 27**

(b) 45　　(c) 63　　(d) 81　　(e) 90

(f) 18　　(g) 36　　(h) 54　　(i) 72

3. Try these.

(a) 3 x 9 = **9 + 9 + 9**　　(b) 2 x 9 = _____　　(c) 4 x 9 = _____

(d) 6 x 9 = _____　　(e) 8 x 9 = _____

(f) 9 x 9 = _____

4. How many squares in

(a) 2 bars? ____　　(b) 3 bars? ____　　(c) 7 bars? ____

(d) 9 bars? ____　　(e) 10 bars? ____　　(f) 5 bars? ____

5. Try these.

(a) 5 x 9 = **45**　　(b) 7 x 9 = ____　　(c) 9 x 9 = ____　　(d) 3 x 9 = ____

(e) 8 x 9 = ____　　(f) 6 x 9 = ____　　(g) 2 x 9 = ____　　(h) 10 x 9 = ____

6. Now try these.

(a) 9　　(b) 9　　(c) 9　　(d) 9　　(e) 9　　(f) 9

　x 3　　　x 9　　　x 5　　　x 10　　　x 4　　　x 6

___　　　___　　　___　　　___　　　___　　　___

58

Problems for you to solve

1. This window has 9 panes of glass.
How many panes of glass in 8 windows? _____

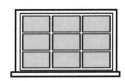

2.  A lollipop costs 9c. Ann bought 6 lollipops.
How much did she pay for them? _____

3. Shane's big brother spends €9 on bus fares
to school every day. How much does it cost
him to travel to school for the week? _____

4.  Mary saw 6 fishing boats moored in the harbour.
There was a crew of 9 people on board each boat.
How many people altogether were on the
6 boats? _____

Target Practice

Look at this target and see if you can find the missing numbers.
9 x 4 = 36 has been filled in to help you.

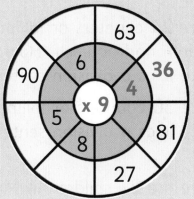

Blow the Horn

This is a simple counting game. The pupils stand around in a
circle and the first pupil calls out the number 1, the second
pupil the number 2, and so on, round the group. But every
time a multiple of 9 is reached, the pupil must call out **BEEP**.
When a pupil makes a mistake they should drop out. The last
remaining pupil in the circle is the winner.

You need:
- counters or lollipop sticks
- to practise division facts 3, 6, 9

Dividing by 3

1. Share these acorns equally among the three children. Draw the acorns on the ground in front of them and then colour them.

(a) How many acorns are there altogether? _____
(b) How many children are there? _____
(c) How many acorns did each child get? _____

A division sentence is written like this: $18 \div 3 = 6$
The symbol $\div$ means 'shared' or 'divided'.

2. Share 24 counters or lollipop sticks equally among two other children and yourself. **How many does each of you get?** _____
Write it as a division sentence ___ $\div$ ___ = _____

Share 30 counters or lollipop sticks in the same way.
Write it as a division sentence ___ $\div$ ___ = _____

3. There are 27 children in Mr O'Reilly's class. He brought them to the swimming pool and divided them into groups of 3.
How many groups were there? _____
Write it as a division sentence ___ $\div$ ___ = _____

4. Use counters to do these.
(a) $12 \div 3 =$ _____ (b) $18 \div 3 =$ _____ (c) $15 \div 3 =$ _____ (d) $6 \div 3 =$ ___
(e) $21 \div 3 =$ _____ (f) $9 \div 3 =$ _____ (g) $3 \div 3 =$ _____ (h) $30 \div 3 =$ ___

Dividing by 6

1. It was sports day at St Paul's school. The principal asked some boys and girls to help her mark out a racing track with cones. She shared the cones among them equally.

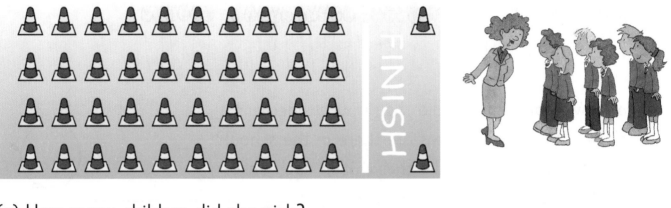

   (a) How many children did she pick? _____
   (b) How many cones were there? _____
   (c) How many did each child get? _____
   (d) Write it as a division sentence _____ ÷ _____ = _____

2. This man is packing these eggs into boxes before delivering them to the supermarket.
   (a) How many eggs are there altogether? _____
   (b) How many eggs fit into each box? _____
   (c) How many boxes will he need? _____
   (d) Write it as a division sentence _____ ÷ _____ = _____

3. Share 36 counters or lollipop sticks equally among five other children and yourself. How many does each of you get? _____
   Write it as a division sentence _____ ÷ _____ = _____
   Share 48 counters or lollipop sticks in the same way.
   Write it as a division sentence _____ ÷ _____ = _____

4. Try these.
   (a) 12 ÷ 6 = _____   (b) 18 ÷ 6 = _____   (c) 36 ÷ 6 = _____   (d) 30 ÷ 6 = _____
   (e) 6 ÷ 6 = _____   (f) 60 ÷ 6 = _____   (g) 54 ÷ 6 = _____   (h) 42 ÷ 6 = _____

Dividing by 9

1. There are some very important visitors coming to visit St Colmcille's School. The teachers bought some flowers to decorate the classrooms. There are 9 classrooms in the school. They shared the flowers equally among the 9 classrooms, with each room getting one vase of flowers.

   (a) How many flowers did they buy altogether? ___

   (b) How many classrooms are there in the school? ___

   (c) How many flowers did they put in each vase? ___

   (d) Write it as a division sentence ___ ÷ ___ = ___

   (e) With your pencil draw the flowers for the vase above and colour them.

2. Annette bought a large pack of sweets when she was on holidays in Spain. When she came home she shared them equally among her friends. She put them into a small paper bag to give to each child.

   (a) How many sweets in the pack altogether? ____

   (b) How many paper bags will she need? ____

   (c) How many sweets will she put in each bag? ____

   (d) Write it as a division sentence ___ ÷ ___ = ____

3. Share 36 counters or lollipop sticks equally among eight other children and yourself. How many does each of you get? _____
   Write it as a division sentence _____ ÷ _____ = _____
   Share 45 counters or lollipop sticks in the same way.
   Write it as a division sentence _____ ÷ _____ = _____

4. Try these.
   (a) 27 ÷ 9 = ___   (b) 18 ÷ 9 = _____   (c) 54 ÷ 9 = _____   (d) 81 ÷ 9 = ____
   (e) 9 ÷ 9 = ___   (f) 90 ÷ 9 = _____   (g) 72 ÷ 9 = _____   (h) 63 ÷ 9 = ____

Dividing by 3, 6, 9

1. 27 books are to be put onto 3 shelves. The same number of books goes on each shelf.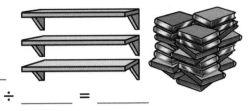
   (a) How many books will go on each shelf? _____
   (b) Write this story as a division sentence. _____ ÷ _____ = _____

2.  If 54 markers were divided equally among 6 children, how many markers would each child have? _____

3. 72 children from third and fourth class were divided into groups of 9 for the school sports. How many groups were there altogether? _____

4.  Paul's grandfather is 81 years of age. Paul is 9 times younger than his grandfather. How old is Paul? Write it as a division sentence.
   _____ ÷ _____ = _____

5. Match the correct numbers in each set.

÷ 3		÷ 6		÷ 9	
15	8	48	6	63	7
30	10	36	10	90	6
24	5	60	8	54	10

Release the Prisoner

Here are 10 keys with questions written on them. You need 4 keys to open the dungeon door and release the prisoner. Work out the answers to the questions on each key and choose the keys that give the answers on the locks. Put the keys you chose on the keyring.

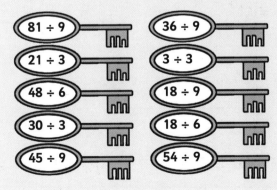
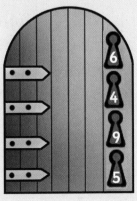

63

Chapter 13
Number patterns

You need:
- rulers
- pencils and colouring pencils

1. Continue the patterns.

   (a) 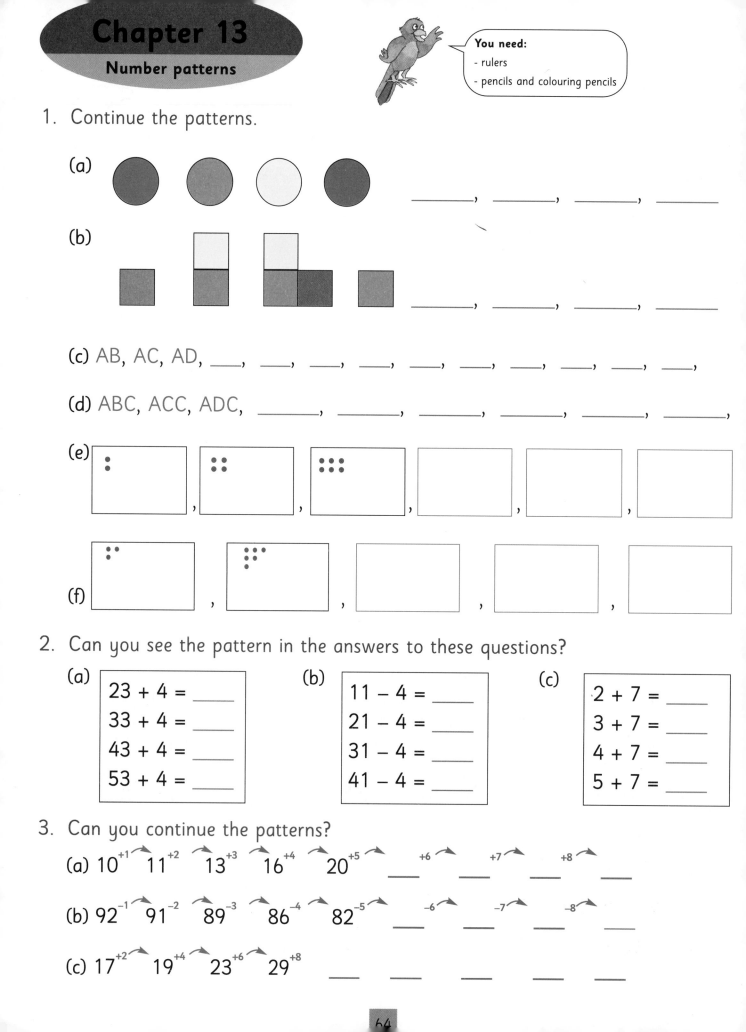 _____, _____, _____, _____

   (b) _____, _____, _____, _____

   (c) AB, AC, AD, ____, ____, ____, ____, ____, ____, ____, ____, ____, ____,

   (d) ABC, ACC, ADC, _____, _____, _____, _____, _____, _____,

   (e)

   (f)

2. Can you see the pattern in the answers to these questions?

   (a)
   23 + 4 = ____
   33 + 4 = ____
   43 + 4 = ____
   53 + 4 = ____

   (b)
   11 − 4 = ____
   21 − 4 = ____
   31 − 4 = ____
   41 − 4 = ____

   (c)
   2 + 7 = ____
   3 + 7 = ____
   4 + 7 = ____
   5 + 7 = ____

3. Can you continue the patterns?

   (a) $10 \overset{+1}{\nearrow} 11 \overset{+2}{\nearrow} 13 \overset{+3}{\nearrow} 16 \overset{+4}{\nearrow} 20 \overset{+5}{\nearrow}$ ____ $\overset{+6}{\nearrow}$ ____ $\overset{+7}{\nearrow}$ ____ $\overset{+8}{\nearrow}$ ____

   (b) $92 \overset{-1}{\nearrow} 91 \overset{-2}{\nearrow} 89 \overset{-3}{\nearrow} 86 \overset{-4}{\nearrow} 82 \overset{-5}{\nearrow}$ ____ $\overset{-6}{\nearrow}$ ____ $\overset{-7}{\nearrow}$ ____ $\overset{-8}{\nearrow}$ ____

   (c) $17 \overset{+2}{\nearrow} 19 \overset{+4}{\nearrow} 23 \overset{+6}{\nearrow} 29 \overset{+8}{\nearrow}$ ____ ____ ____

Pattern

1. Look at these number patterns. Can you continue them?

(a) 2, 4, 6, 8, ___, ___, ___, ___, ___, ___, ___, ___

(b) 3, 6, 9, 12, ___, ___, ___, ___, ___, ___, ___, ___

(c) 5, 10, 15, 20, ___, ___, ___, ___, ___, ___, ___, ___

(d) 4, 8, 12, ___, ___, ___, ___, ___, ___, ___, ___

(e) 60, 54, 48, ___, ___, ___, ___, ___, ___, ___, ___

(f) 100, 90, 80, ___, ___, ___, ___, ___, ___, ___, ___

(g) 90, 81, 72, ___, ___, ___, ___, ___, ___, ___, ___

2. Find the missing numbers in these patterns.

(a) 1, 3, 5, 7, ___, ___, ___, ___, ___, ___, ___, ___

(b) 1, 4, 7, 10, ___, ___, ___, ___, ___, ___, ___, ___

(c) 1, 3, 6, 10, ___, ___, ___, ___, ___, ___, ___, ___

(d) 1, 4, 9, 16, ___, ___, ___, ___, ___, ___, ___, ___

(e) 5c, 9c, 14c, 20c, ___, ___, ___, ___, ___, ___, ___, ___

(f) 82, 81, 79, 76, ___, ___, ___, ___, ___, ___, ___, ___

(g) 100, 98, 94, 88, ___, ___, ___, ___, ___, ___, ___

3. Complete these big number patterns.

(a) 115, 119, 123, ___, ___, ___, ___, ___, ___, ___, ___

(b) 479, 484, 489, ___, ___, ___, ___, ___, ___, ___, ___

(c) 891, 898, 905, ___, ___, ___, ___, ___, ___, ___, ___

(d) 620, 611, 602, ___, ___, ___, ___, ___, ___, ___, ___

Fun on the Patio

Mr Joyce is building a new patio with these paving slabs. He has already started the pattern. Continue the pattern by drawing the other paving slabs and then colour them in.
The dotted lines will help you to get started.

(a)

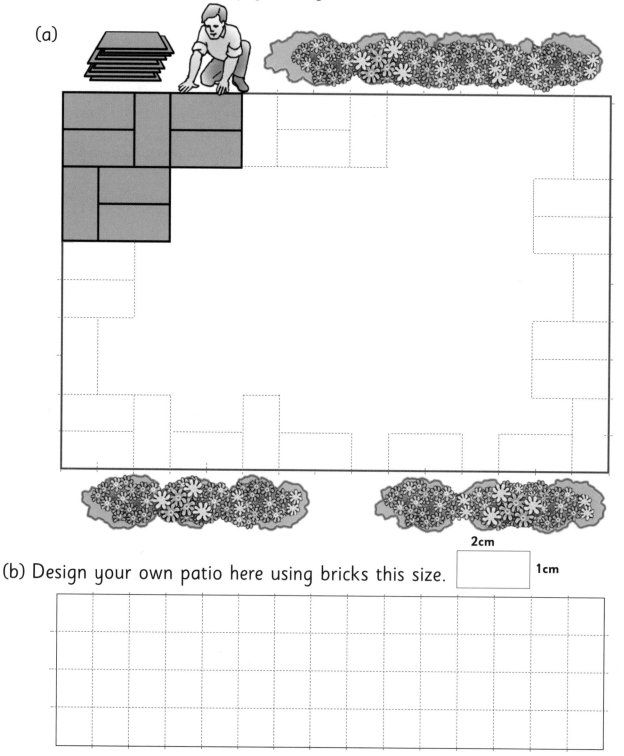

(b) Design your own patio here using bricks this size.

2cm
1cm

(c) Colour the bricks to finish your design.

Chapter 14

Time to look back 3

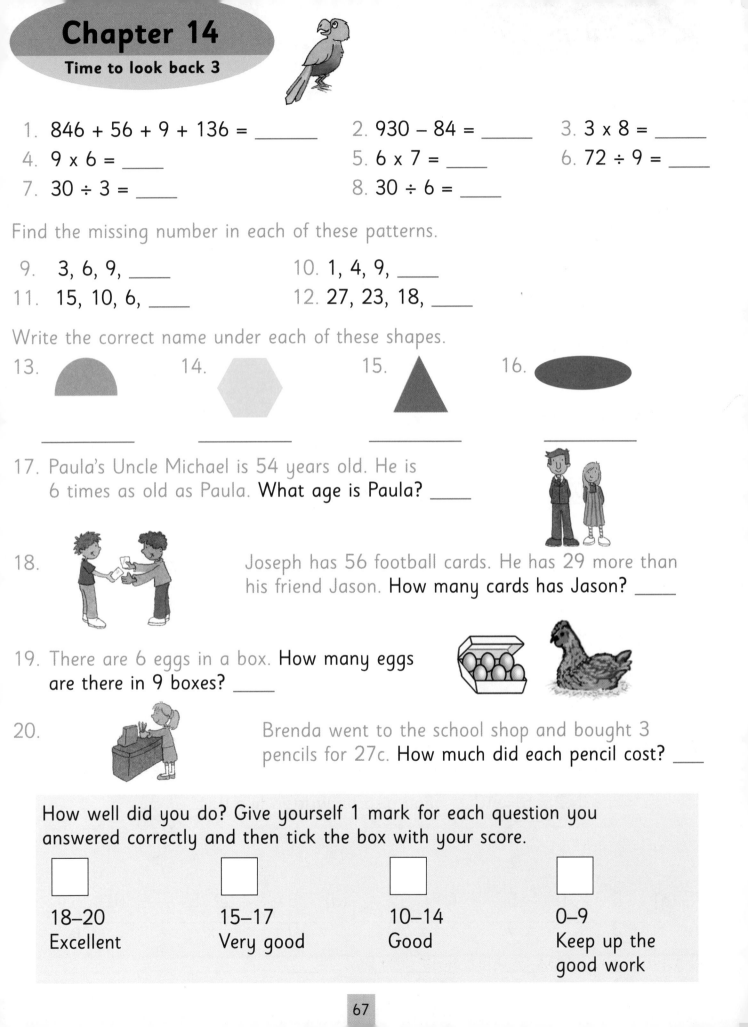

1. 846 + 56 + 9 + 136 = _____   2. 930 – 84 = _____   3. 3 x 8 = _____
4. 9 x 6 = _____   5. 6 x 7 = _____   6. 72 ÷ 9 = _____
7. 30 ÷ 3 = _____   8. 30 ÷ 6 = _____

Find the missing number in each of these patterns.

9. 3, 6, 9, _____   10. 1, 4, 9, _____
11. 15, 10, 6, _____   12. 27, 23, 18, _____

Write the correct name under each of these shapes.

13.   14.   15.   16.

_____   _____   _____   _____

17. Paula's Uncle Michael is 54 years old. He is
    6 times as old as Paula. **What age is Paula?** _____

18.   Joseph has 56 football cards. He has 29 more than
    his friend Jason. **How many cards has Jason?** _____

19. There are 6 eggs in a box. **How many eggs
    are there in 9 boxes?** _____

20.   Brenda went to the school shop and bought 3
    pencils for 27c. **How much did each pencil cost?** ___

How well did you do? Give yourself 1 mark for each question you
answered correctly and then tick the box with your score.

☐   ☐   ☐   ☐

18–20   15–17   10–14   0–9
Excellent   Very good   Good   Keep up the
                                   good work

You need:
- to practise multiplication facts 5 and 10

Multiplying by 5

1. Help Joey to reach 50. Circle the numbers he will land on.

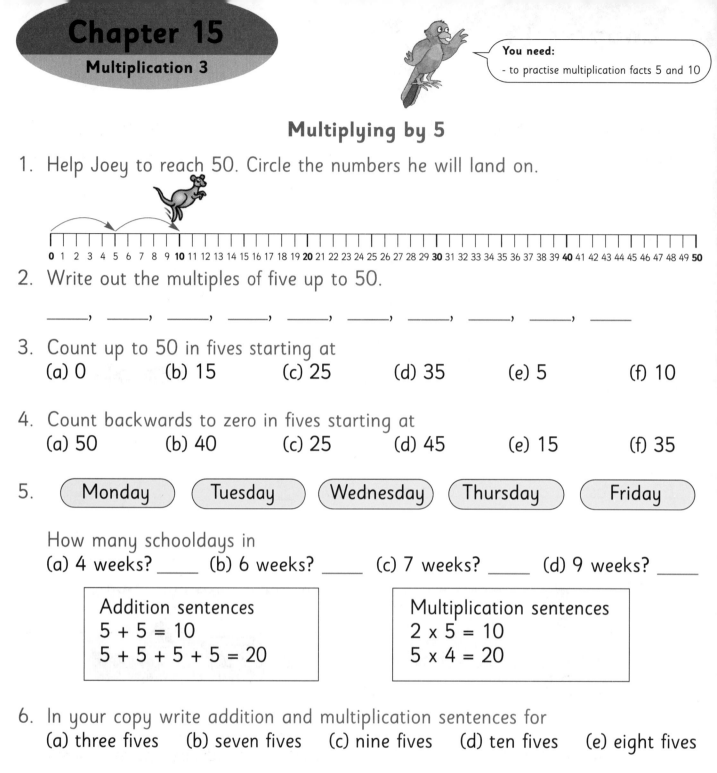

0 1 2 3 4 5 6 7 8 9 **10** 11 12 13 14 15 16 17 18 19 **20** 21 22 23 24 25 26 27 28 29 **30** 31 32 33 34 35 36 37 38 39 **40** 41 42 43 44 45 46 47 48 49 **50**

2. Write out the multiples of five up to 50.

_____, _____, _____, _____, _____, _____, _____, _____, _____, _____

3. Count up to 50 in fives starting at
   (a) 0   (b) 15   (c) 25   (d) 35   (e) 5   (f) 10

4. Count backwards to zero in fives starting at
   (a) 50   (b) 40   (c) 25   (d) 45   (e) 15   (f) 35

5. (Monday)   (Tuesday)   (Wednesday)   (Thursday)   (Friday)

   How many schooldays in
   (a) 4 weeks? _____   (b) 6 weeks? _____   (c) 7 weeks? _____   (d) 9 weeks? _____

Addition sentences	Multiplication sentences
5 + 5 = 10	2 x 5 = 10
5 + 5 + 5 + 5 = 20	5 x 4 = 20

6. In your copy write addition and multiplication sentences for
   (a) three fives   (b) seven fives   (c) nine fives   (d) ten fives   (e) eight fives

   (2 x 5 = 10)   may also be written like this

   ```
     5
   x 2
   ----
    10
   ```

7. (a)   5   (b)   5   (c)   5   (d)   5   (e)   5   (f)   5
        x 3   x 9   x 5   x 10   x 4   x 6
        ____   ____   ____   ____   ____   ____

        ____   ____   ____   ____   ____   ____

Multiplying by 5

1. Fill in the blanks.

   (a) 3 x 5 = __   (b) __ x 5 = 35   (c) __ x 5 = 50   (d) __ x 5 = 30

   (e) 4 x __ = 20   (f) __ x 5 = 25   (g) __ x 5 = 40   (h) __ x 5 = 0

School Quiz

2. Five children sat at each table for the quiz. How many chairs were needed for

   (a) 2 tables?____   (b) 7 tables?____   (c) 5 tables?____   (d) 8 tables?____

3. Each child got a chocolate bar at the end of the quiz. How many bars were needed for

   (a) 4 teams?____   (b) 3 teams?____   (c) 10 teams?____   (d) 6 teams?____

4. Each correct answer was worth 5 points. Fill in the teams' scores.

Team	A	B	C	D	E	F	G	H	I	J
Number of correct answers	8	7	10	3	9	7	5	6	2	4
Score										

Which team came first? ____   second? ____   third? ____

The Hungry Snail

This snail is hungry and wants to eat the lovely green leaves on the flowers. Colour the multiples of five to show him the path to the flowers.

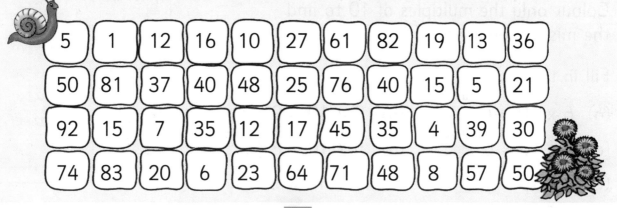

5	1	12	16	10	27	61	82	19	13	36
50	81	37	40	48	25	76	40	15	5	21
92	15	7	35	12	17	45	35	4	39	30
74	83	20	6	23	64	71	48	8	57	50

Multiplying by 10

1.

1	2	3	4	5	6	7	8	9	10
11	12	13	14	15	16	17	18	19	20
21	22	23	24	25	26	27	28	29	30
31	32	33	34	35	36	37	38	39	40
42	42	43	44	45	46	47	48	49	50
51	52	53	54	55	56	57	58	59	60
61	62	63	64	65	66	67	68	69	70
71	72	73	74	75	76	77	78	79	80
81	82	83	84	85	86	87	88	89	90
91	92	93	94	95	96	97	98	99	100

Count in tens and colour the multiples of ten on this hundred square.

Write the multiples of ten here.

_____, _____, _____, _____, _____,

_____, _____, _____, _____, _____

2. Do these addition and multiplication sentences.

(a) 10 + 10 + 10 = 3 x __ = __

(b) 10 + __ + __ + __ + __ = __ x __ = __

3. In your copy write multiplication and addition sentences for

(a) four tens   (b) six tens   (c) eight tens   (d) seven tens   (e) ten tens

4.

(a) 10
    x 2
    ___

(b) 10
    x 4
    ___

(c) 10
    x 5
    ___

(d) 10
    x 9
    ___

(e) 10
    x 10
    ___

(f) 10
    x 6
    ___

5. Ms Collins collected €10 from each child to pay for a trip to an adventure park. How much did she collect from

(a) 9 children? _____   (b) 7 children? _____

(c) 5 children? _____   (d) 8 children? _____

6. Colour only the multiples of 10 to find the missing number.

7. Fill in the blanks.

(a) 6 x 10 = 6 _ (t u)   (b) 9 x 10 = 9 _ (t u)

(c) 8 x 10 = 8 _ (t u)   (d) 5 x 10 = 8 _ (t u)

(e) 3 x 10 = 3 _ (t u)   (f) 10 x 10 = 3 _ (t u)

17	23	19	47	91	86	73	4
7	10	27	80	10	20	40	19
14	40	16	90	76	32	60	16
27	50	98	70	26	19	70	27
8	70	99	50	63	84	90	46
16	90	63	40	96	27	10	59
64	10	59	20	50	60	30	23
71	92	43	28	61	54	87	99

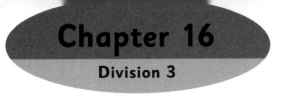

You need:
- counters/lollipop sticks
- to practise division facts 5 and 10
- colouring pencils/markers

Dividing by 5

1. Share these apples equally among the five children. Use your pencil to draw the apples on the table in front of them and then colour them.

   (a) How many apples are there altogether? ___

   (b) How many children are there? ___

   (c) How many apples did each child get? ___

   (d) Write it as a division sentence ___ ÷ ___ = ___

2. Share 40 counters or lollipop sticks equally among four other children and yourself. How many does each of you get? ___
Write it as a division sentence ___ ÷ ___ = ___
Share 50 counters or lollipop sticks in the same way.
Write it as a division sentence ___ ÷ ___ = ___

3. There are 30 children in Ballymore Youth Club. The leader brought them on an outing to the Wicklow Mountains and divided them into groups of 5.

   (a) How many groups were there? ___

   (b) Write it as a division sentence ___ ÷ ___ = ___

4. Use counters or lollipop sticks to do the following questions.

   (a) $20 ÷ 5 =$ ___   (b) $30 ÷ 5 =$ ___   (c) $25 ÷ 5 =$ ___   (d) $10 ÷ 5 =$ ___

   (e) $35 ÷ 5 =$ ___   (f) $15 ÷ 5 =$ ___   (g) $5 ÷ 5 =$ ___   (h) $50 ÷ 5 =$ ___

Dividing by 10

1. These 10 children were on the winning team at the Sports Day in St Paul's School. These bars were shared among them equally as a prize.

   (a) How many children were on the team? ___

   (b) How many bars were there to be shared? ___

   (c) How many bars did each child get? ___

   (d) Write it as a division sentence ___ ÷ ___ = ___

2. This man is packing computer CDs into boxes in the factory before delivering them to the computer shop.

   (a) How many CDs are there altogether? ___

   (b) How many CDs fit into each box? ___

   (c) How many boxes will he need? ___

   (d) Write it as a division sentence ___ ÷ ___ = ___

3. Share 40 counters or lollipop sticks equally among 9 other children and yourself. How many does each of you get? ___
   Write it as a division sentence ___ ÷ ___ = ___
   Share 60 counters or lollipop sticks in the same way.
   Write it as a division sentence ___ ÷ ___ = ___

4. Try these.

   (a) 20 ÷ 10 = ___   (b) 30 ÷ 10 = ___   (c) 90 ÷ 10 = ___   (d) 50 ÷ 10 = ___

   (e) 10 ÷ 10 = ___   (f) 100 ÷ 10 = ___   (g) 80 ÷ 10 = ___   (h) 70 ÷ 10 = ___

Problems for you to solve

1. The teacher gave 4 packs of markers to a group of 5 children doing a project. There were 10 markers in each pack. The children shared the markers equally among themselves.
How many did each child get? _____
Write it as a division sentence ____ ÷ ____ = ____

2.  A shopkeeper bought a box of 45 oranges. He put them into plastic bags with 5 oranges in each bag. How many bags did he need? _____

3. There are 10 tennis balls in a box. How many boxes can be filled if there are 90 balls? _____

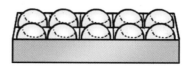

4. 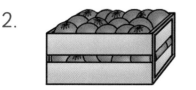 How many teams of 10-a-side can be made from 70 players? _____

5. Read what is written on each box and answer the questions below.

(a) 10 children shared the pencils among them.
How many did each child get? _____

(b) Michael spent 40c on lollipops. How many did he buy? _____

(c) Susan spent €1 on chocolate bars. How many did she buy? _____

(d) How many groups of 5 could I make from the rulers? _____

(e) How many groups of 10 could I make from the sharpeners? _____

(f) Aoife went to the school shop with 80c to buy erasers for some children in her class. How many erasers could she buy? _____

Chapter 17

Fractions 2

Tenths

1. This rectangle is divided into 10 equal parts.

   | $\frac{1}{10}$ | $\frac{1}{10}$ | $\frac{1}{10}$ | $\frac{1}{10}$ | $\frac{1}{10}$ | $\frac{1}{10}$ | $\frac{1}{10}$ | $\frac{1}{10}$ | $\frac{1}{10}$ | $\frac{1}{10}$ |

   Each part is called **one tenth or** $\frac{1}{10}$.
   Fold your rectangle into 10 equal parts.
   Write $\frac{1}{10}$ on each tenth and colour your rectangle.

2. What fraction of these rectangles is coloured?

   (a) 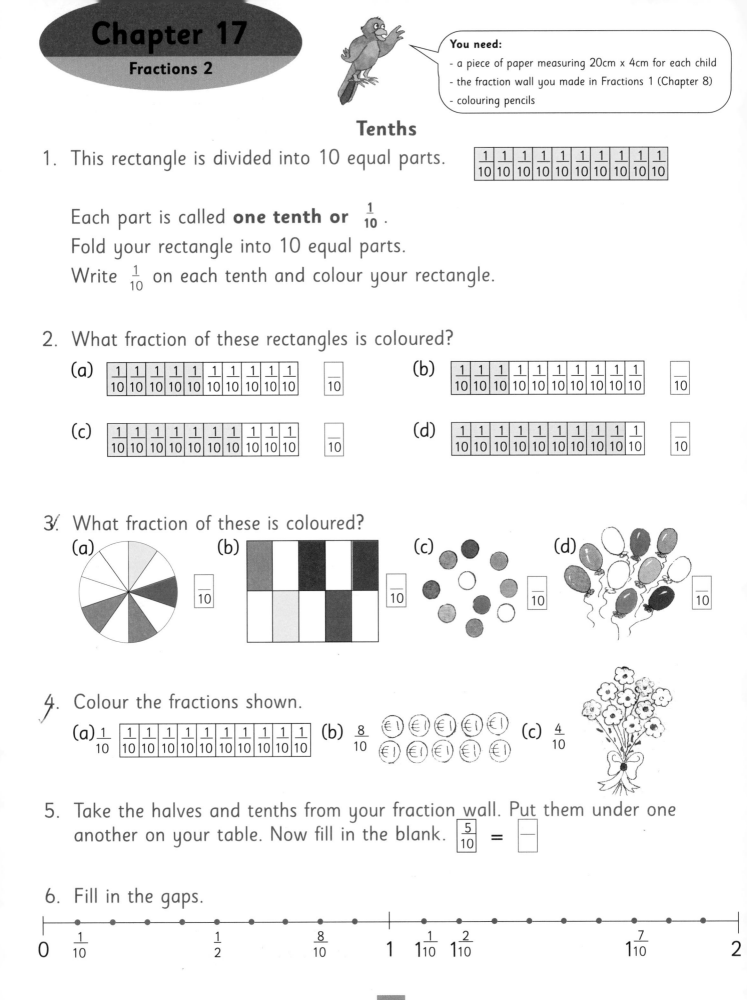 $\frac{}{10}$

   (b) $\frac{}{10}$

   (c) $\frac{}{10}$

   (d) $\frac{}{10}$

3. What fraction of these is coloured?

   (a) $\frac{}{10}$ (b) $\frac{}{10}$ (c) $\frac{}{10}$ (d) $\frac{}{10}$

4. Colour the fractions shown.

   (a) $\frac{1}{10}$ (b) $\frac{8}{10}$ (c) $\frac{4}{10}$

5. Take the halves and tenths from your fraction wall. Put them under one another on your table. Now fill in the blank. $\frac{5}{10} = \frac{}{}$

6. Fill in the gaps.

   0    $\frac{1}{10}$ $\frac{1}{2}$ $\frac{8}{10}$ 1 $1\frac{1}{10}$ $1\frac{2}{10}$ $1\frac{7}{10}$ 2

Finding $\frac{1}{2}$ of a number

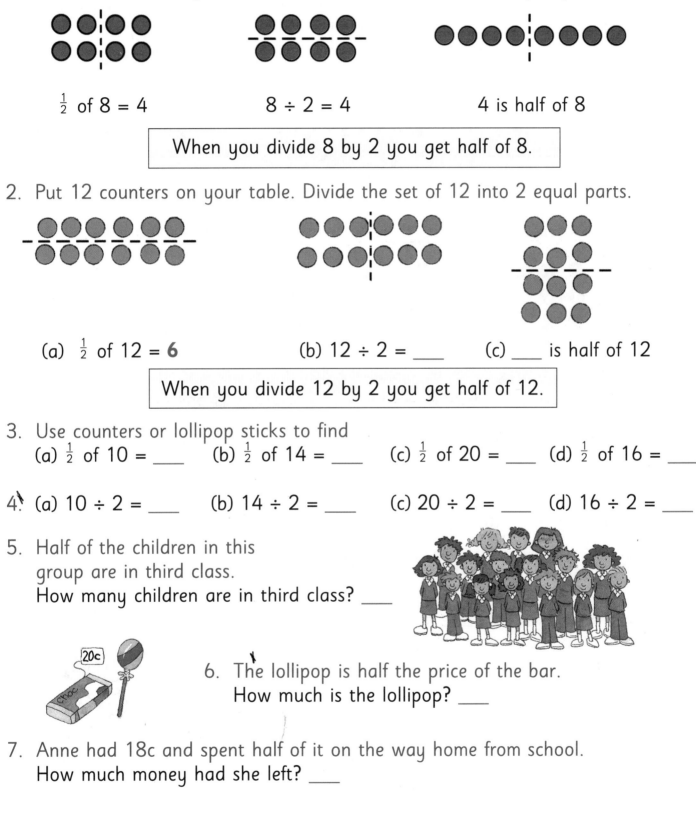

1. Put 8 counters on your table. Divide the set of 8 into 2 equal parts.

    $\frac{1}{2}$ of 8 = 4   8 ÷ 2 = 4   4 is half of 8

    > When you divide 8 by 2 you get half of 8.

2. Put 12 counters on your table. Divide the set of 12 into 2 equal parts.

    (a) $\frac{1}{2}$ of 12 = **6**   (b) 12 ÷ 2 = ___   (c) ___ is half of 12

    > When you divide 12 by 2 you get half of 12.

3. Use counters or lollipop sticks to find
    (a) $\frac{1}{2}$ of 10 = ___   (b) $\frac{1}{2}$ of 14 = ___   (c) $\frac{1}{2}$ of 20 = ___   (d) $\frac{1}{2}$ of 16 = ___

4. (a) 10 ÷ 2 = ___   (b) 14 ÷ 2 = ___   (c) 20 ÷ 2 = ___   (d) 16 ÷ 2 = ___

5. Half of the children in this
    group are in third class.
    How many children are in third class? ___

6. The lollipop is half the price of the bar.
    How much is the lollipop? ___

7. Anne had 18c and spent half of it on the way home from school.
    How much money had she left? ___

> **Remember: To find $\frac{1}{2}$ a number divide by 2.**

75

Finding $\frac{1}{4}$ of a number

1. Put 8 counters on your table. Make 4 equal sets.

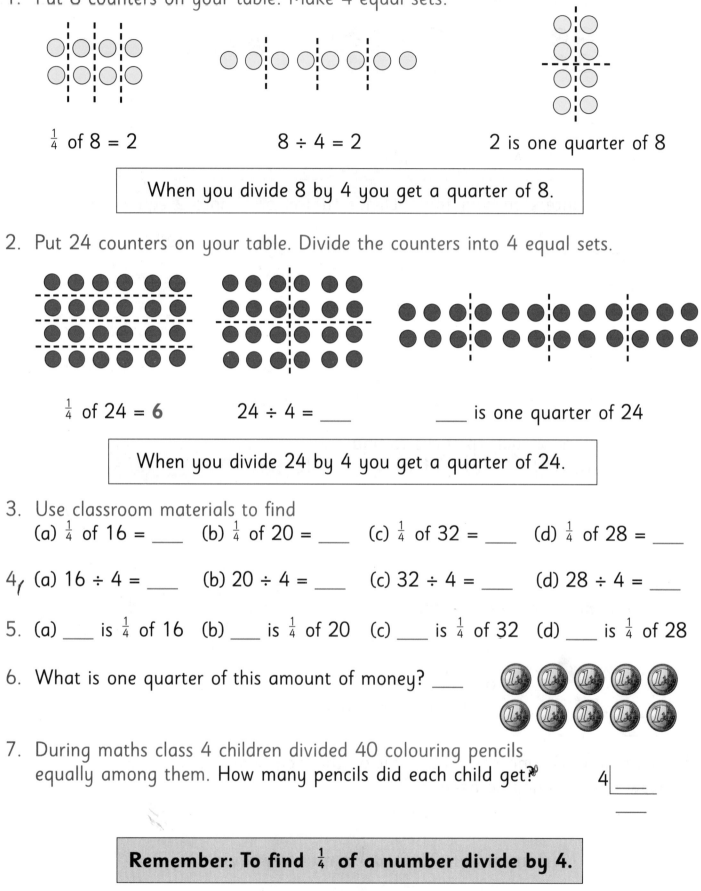

$\frac{1}{4}$ of 8 = 2   8 ÷ 4 = 2   2 is one quarter of 8

> When you divide 8 by 4 you get a quarter of 8.

2. Put 24 counters on your table. Divide the counters into 4 equal sets.

$\frac{1}{4}$ of 24 = **6**   24 ÷ 4 = ___   ___ is one quarter of 24

> When you divide 24 by 4 you get a quarter of 24.

3. Use classroom materials to find
   (a) $\frac{1}{4}$ of 16 = ___   (b) $\frac{1}{4}$ of 20 = ___   (c) $\frac{1}{4}$ of 32 = ___   (d) $\frac{1}{4}$ of 28 = ___

4. (a) 16 ÷ 4 = ___   (b) 20 ÷ 4 = ___   (c) 32 ÷ 4 = ___   (d) 28 ÷ 4 = ___

5. (a) ___ is $\frac{1}{4}$ of 16   (b) ___ is $\frac{1}{4}$ of 20   (c) ___ is $\frac{1}{4}$ of 32   (d) ___ is $\frac{1}{4}$ of 28

6. What is one quarter of this amount of money? ___

7. During maths class 4 children divided 40 colouring pencils equally among them. How many pencils did each child get?

$4\underline{}$

> **Remember: To find $\frac{1}{4}$ of a number divide by 4.**

Finding $\frac{1}{8}$ of a number

1. Put 16 counters on your table. Make 8 equal sets.

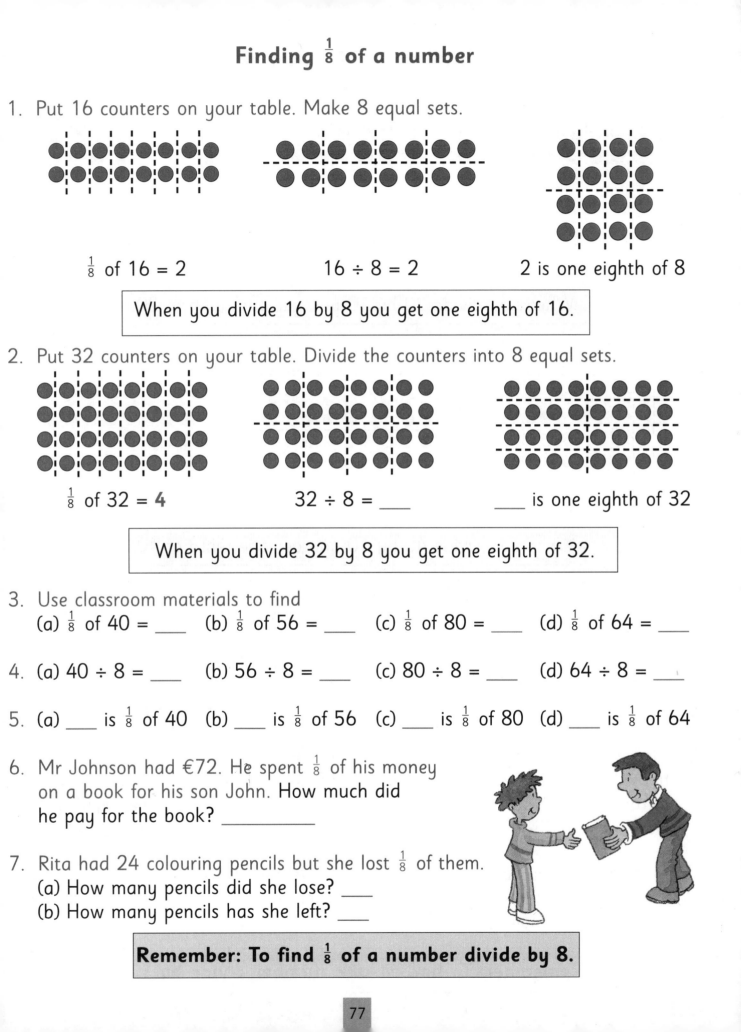

$\frac{1}{8}$ of 16 = 2   16 ÷ 8 = 2   2 is one eighth of 8

When you divide 16 by 8 you get one eighth of 16.

2. Put 32 counters on your table. Divide the counters into 8 equal sets.

$\frac{1}{8}$ of 32 = **4**   32 ÷ 8 = ___   ___ is one eighth of 32

When you divide 32 by 8 you get one eighth of 32.

3. Use classroom materials to find
   (a) $\frac{1}{8}$ of 40 = ___   (b) $\frac{1}{8}$ of 56 = ___   (c) $\frac{1}{8}$ of 80 = ___   (d) $\frac{1}{8}$ of 64 = ___

4. (a) 40 ÷ 8 = ___   (b) 56 ÷ 8 = ___   (c) 80 ÷ 8 = ___   (d) 64 ÷ 8 = ___

5. (a) ___ is $\frac{1}{8}$ of 40   (b) ___ is $\frac{1}{8}$ of 56   (c) ___ is $\frac{1}{8}$ of 80   (d) ___ is $\frac{1}{8}$ of 64

6. Mr Johnson had €72. He spent $\frac{1}{8}$ of his money
   on a book for his son John. How much did
   he pay for the book? _____

7. Rita had 24 colouring pencils but she lost $\frac{1}{8}$ of them.
   (a) How many pencils did she lose? ___
   (b) How many pencils has she left? ___

Remember: To find $\frac{1}{8}$ of a number divide by 8.

Finding $\frac{1}{10}$ of a number

1. Put 20 counters on your table. Make 10 equal sets.

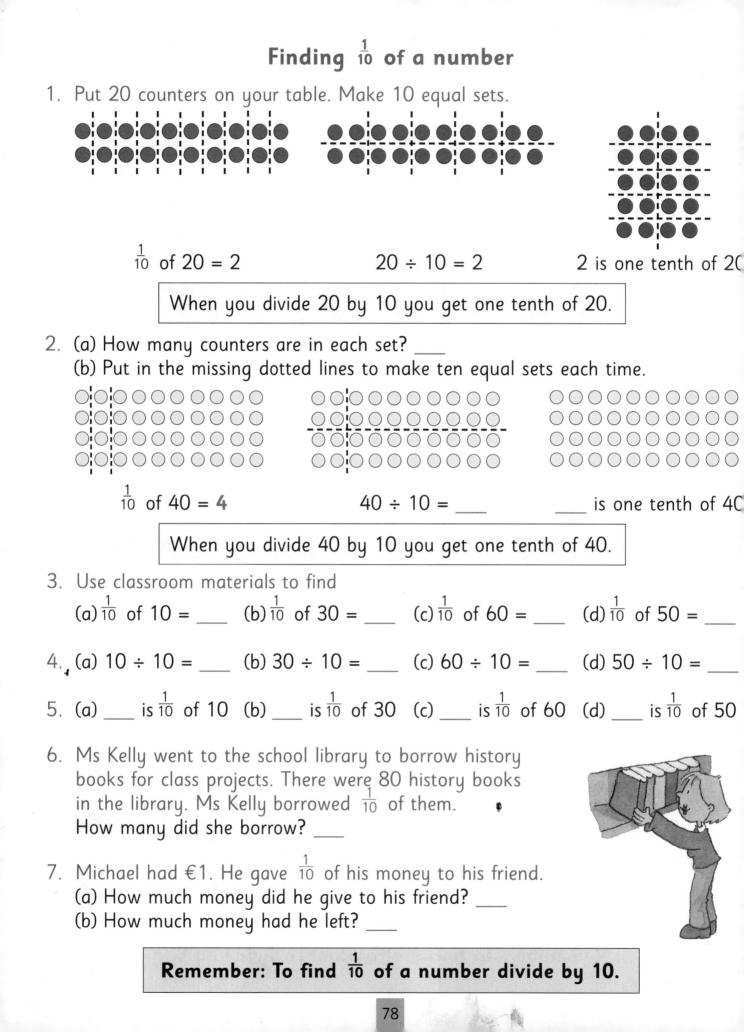

$\frac{1}{10}$ of 20 = 2   20 ÷ 10 = 2   2 is one tenth of 20

> When you divide 20 by 10 you get one tenth of 20.

2. (a) How many counters are in each set? ___
   (b) Put in the missing dotted lines to make ten equal sets each time.

$\frac{1}{10}$ of 40 = **4**   40 ÷ 10 = ___   ___ is one tenth of 40

> When you divide 40 by 10 you get one tenth of 40.

3. Use classroom materials to find
   (a) $\frac{1}{10}$ of 10 = ___   (b) $\frac{1}{10}$ of 30 = ___   (c) $\frac{1}{10}$ of 60 = ___   (d) $\frac{1}{10}$ of 50 = ___

4. (a) 10 ÷ 10 = ___   (b) 30 ÷ 10 = ___   (c) 60 ÷ 10 = ___   (d) 50 ÷ 10 = ___

5. (a) ___ is $\frac{1}{10}$ of 10   (b) ___ is $\frac{1}{10}$ of 30   (c) ___ is $\frac{1}{10}$ of 60   (d) ___ is $\frac{1}{10}$ of 50

6. Ms Kelly went to the school library to borrow history books for class projects. There were 80 history books in the library. Ms Kelly borrowed $\frac{1}{10}$ of them. How many did she borrow? ___

7. Michael had €1. He gave $\frac{1}{10}$ of his money to his friend.
   (a) How much money did he give to his friend? ___
   (b) How much money had he left? ___

> **Remember: To find $\frac{1}{10}$ of a number divide by 10.**

Chapter 18
Decimals

You need:
- colouring pencils

1. What fraction needs to be coloured?

   (a) $\frac{1}{10}$ To be coloured

   (b) ☐ To be coloured

   (c) ☐ To be coloured

   (d) ☐ To be coloured

2. Fill in the tenths and colour.

1 unit

3. (a) How many tenths in 1 unit? $\frac{\ }{10}$ (b) $\frac{5}{10}$ = $\frac{\ }{\ }$

$\frac{1}{10}$ may also be written like this: 0.1

$\frac{1}{10}$ is a **fraction**   0.1 is a **decimal fraction**

---

4. Fill in the missing **fractions** and **decimal fractions** on this number line.

   $\frac{1}{10}$ $\frac{2}{10}$ $\frac{3}{10}$ ($\frac{5}{10}$) $\frac{1}{2}$ $\frac{6}{10}$ $\frac{10}{10}$ 1

   0   0.1   0.2   0.6   1.0

5. (a) $\frac{1}{10}$ = **0.1**   (b) $\frac{2}{10}$ = 0.___   (c) $\frac{3}{10}$ = 0.___   (d) $\frac{6}{10}$ = ___.___   (e) $\frac{10}{10}$ = ___.___

6. What fraction and decimal fractions of these shapes is coloured?

   (a) $\frac{\ }{\ }$ ___.___

   (b) $\frac{\ }{\ }$ ___.___

   (c) $\frac{\ }{\ }$ ___.___

   (d) $\frac{\ }{\ }$ ___.___

   What fraction and decimal fractions of these shapes is not coloured?

   (e) $\frac{\ }{\ }$ ___.___

   (f) $\frac{\ }{\ }$ ___.___

   (g) $\frac{\ }{\ }$ ___.___

   (h) $\frac{\ }{\ }$ ___.___

Decimals

1. Colour the amounts shown.

   (a) 0.3   (b) 0.7   (c) 0.1   (d) $0.5 = \dfrac{\boxed{}}{10} = \dfrac{1}{\boxed{}}$

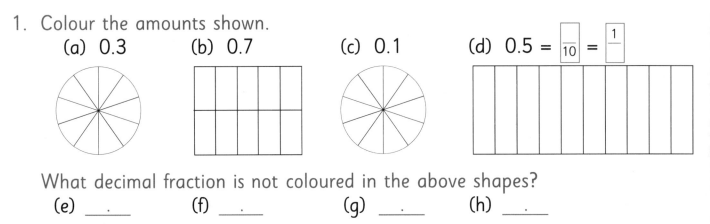

   What decimal fraction is not coloured in the above shapes?

   (e) ___ . ___   (f) ___ . ___   (g) ___ . ___   (h) ___ . ___

2. Look at these pictures. Fill in the missing fractions and decimal fractions on the number line.

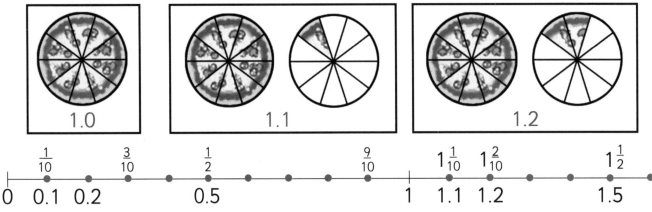

3. Colour the correct amount of pizza.

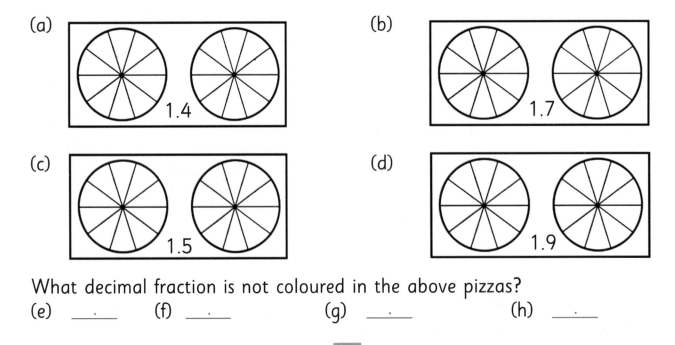

   (a) 1.4   (b) 1.7

   (c) 1.5   (d) 1.9

   What decimal fraction is not coloured in the above pizzas?

   (e) ___ . ___   (f) ___ . ___   (g) ___ . ___   (h) ___ . ___

80

More decimals

1. Look at these strips.

0.5 is red   0.5 is yellow   0.3 is yellow   0.7 is green

Now read what is written under these strips and colour them correctly.

0.2 blue   0.8 yellow   0.4 pink   0.6 red

0.9 orange   0.1 black   0.5 green   0.5 yellow

2. Circle the decimal fraction of **greater** value in each pair.
   (a) 0.4, 0.6   (b) 0.9, 0.1   (c) 0.8, 0.7
   (d) 0.5, 0.7   (e) 0.6, 0.9   (f) 0.3, 0.4

3. Circle the decimal fraction of **lesser** value in each pair.
   (a) 0.9, 0.2   (b) 0.5, 0.6   (c) 0.3, 0.9
   (d) 0.7, 0.5   (e) 0.8, 0.9   (f) 0.6, 0.1

4. When this pizza was delivered to the Ryan family it was in ten equal slices. Richard ate 2 slices. Colour 2 slices in green.
   (a) What decimal fraction has been eaten? ____.____
   (b) What decimal fraction remains? ____.____

   Then Dad came in and had 0.3 of the pizza. Colour the number of slices he ate in red.
   (c) What decimal fraction of the pizza is left now? ____.____

   Mammy ate 2 slices. Colour those two slices yellow.
   (d) What decimal fraction of the pizza has been eaten? ____.____
   (e) What decimal fraction of the pizza remains? ____.____

   Kate brought two friends home and they shared the remaining slices of pizza equally among the three of them. Colour the slices they ate in blue.
   (f) What decimal fraction did each child have? ____.____

Some decimal fun

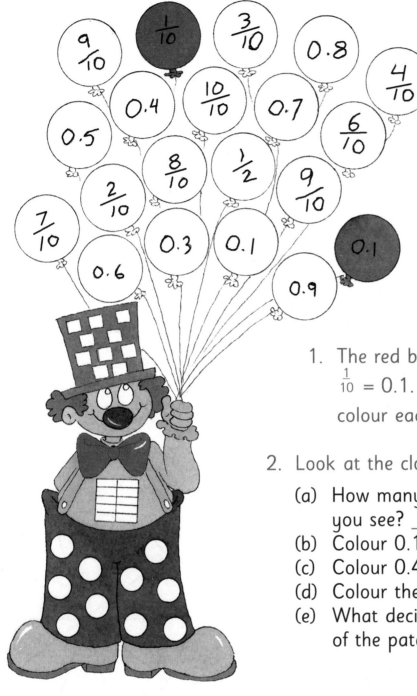

1. The red balloons match because $\frac{1}{10}$ = 0.1. Choose different colours and colour each matching pair of balloons.

2. Look at the clown's hat.
   (a) How many patches can you see? ____
   (b) Colour 0.1 of the patches blue.
   (c) Colour 0.4 of the patches yellow.
   (d) Colour the rest of the patches red.
   (e) What decimal fraction and fraction of the patches are red? ____ . ___ $\boxed{}$

3. Look at the clown's trousers.
   (a) How many circles can you see? ____
   (b) Colour $\frac{1}{2}$ of the circles in blue.
   (c) What decimal fraction of the circles is left to colour? ____ . ___
   (d) Colour the remaining circles.

4. Look at the clown's shirt pocket.
   (a) Colour $\frac{3}{10}$ of the pocket in red.
   (b) Colour 0.5 of the pocket in blue.
   (c) What decimal fraction and fraction is left to colour? ____ . ___ $\boxed{}$
   (d) Finish colouring the pocket in yellow.

82

You need:
- scissors
- tracing paper
- squared paper
- colouring pencils

1. Trace this shape onto a piece of paper and then cut it out.

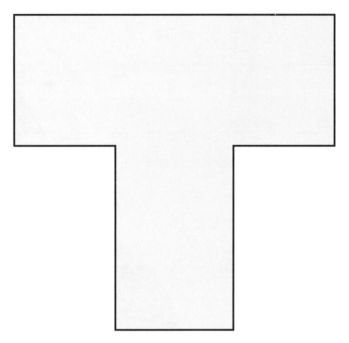

When you have cut it out, fold it in such a way that one half fits exactly on top of the other. Were you able to do it?

This shape is **symmetrical** because you can fold one half exactly on top of the other.

The folding line is called the **line of symmetry**. With your pencil draw the line of symmetry on the shape you have cut out.

2.

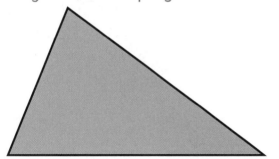

   (a)   What shape is this? _____
   (b)   Do you think it is symmetrical? _____
   (c)   Trace the shape onto a piece of paper and cut it out.
   (d)   Can you find a line of symmetry by folding the shape? _____
   (e)   Put a tick beside the sentence which is true.
         This shape is symmetrical. ☐ This shape is not symmetrical. ☐

Symmetry

Which of these are symmetrical? Put a tick (✔) in the box and draw the lines of symmetry for the shapes that are symmetrical.

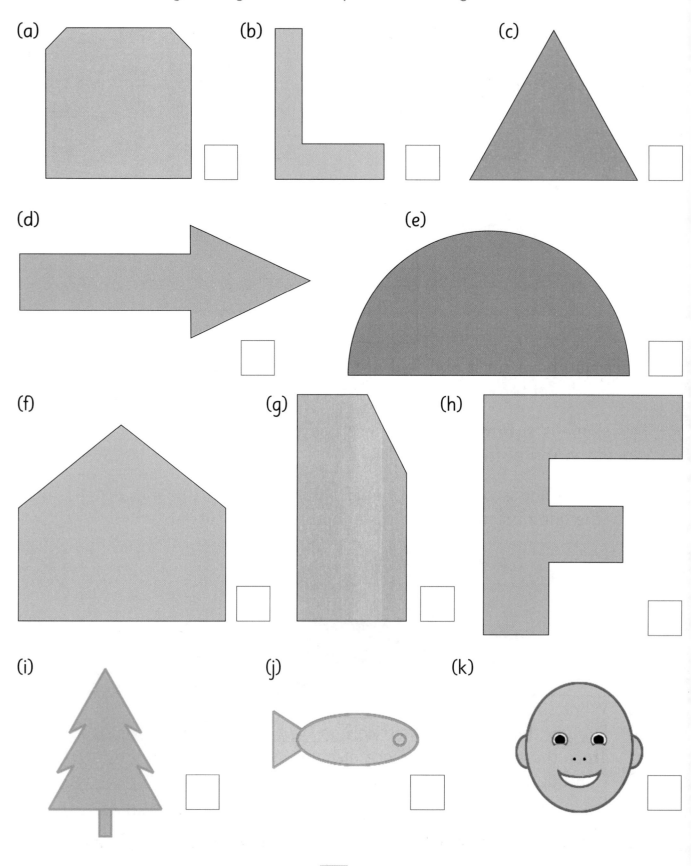

(a)

(b)

(c)

(d)

(e)

(f)

(g)

(h)

(i)

(j)

(k)

Drawing symmetrical shapes

1. Look at the following list of objects. Tick the ones that you think are symmetrical.

   (a) the classroom door ☐   (b) the classroom window ☐
   (c) the kettle ☐   (d) an apple ☐
   (e) a cup ☐   (f) your tracksuit top ☐
   (g) your tracksuit bottom ☐   (h) your jumper ☐
   (i) a dinner plate ☐   (j) a banana ☐

   Draw three of the items that you ticked.

2. Some symmetrical shapes have only one line of symmetry, while others have two or more lines of symmetry.

   Draw the lines of symmetry in these shapes.

How many lines of symmetry? _____   How many lines of symmetry? _____

More lines of symmetry

1. Look at these symmetrical shapes. Draw the lines of symmetry in each one.

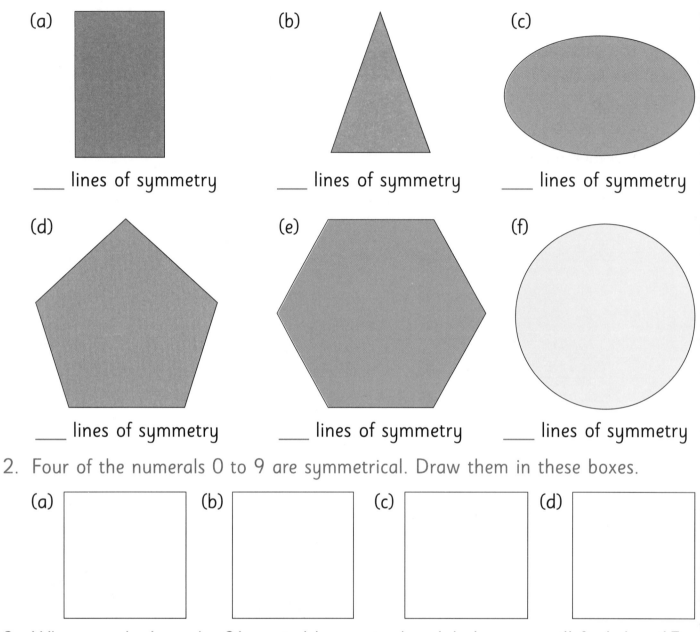

(a) ___ lines of symmetry

(b) ___ lines of symmetry

(c) ___ lines of symmetry

(d) ___ lines of symmetry

(e) ___ lines of symmetry

(f) ___ lines of symmetry

2. Four of the numerals 0 to 9 are symmetrical. Draw them in these boxes.

(a)

(b)

(c)

(d)

3. When you look at the 26 capital letters in the alphabet you will find that 15 of them are symmetrical and 3 of them have **2 or more lines of symmetry**. Can you draw these 3 capital letters and their lines of symmetry in the boxes below? A B C D E F G H I J K L M N O P Q R S T U V W X Y Z

(a)

(b)

(c)

The missing half

Draw the missing half of these symmetrical shapes. Then colour them.

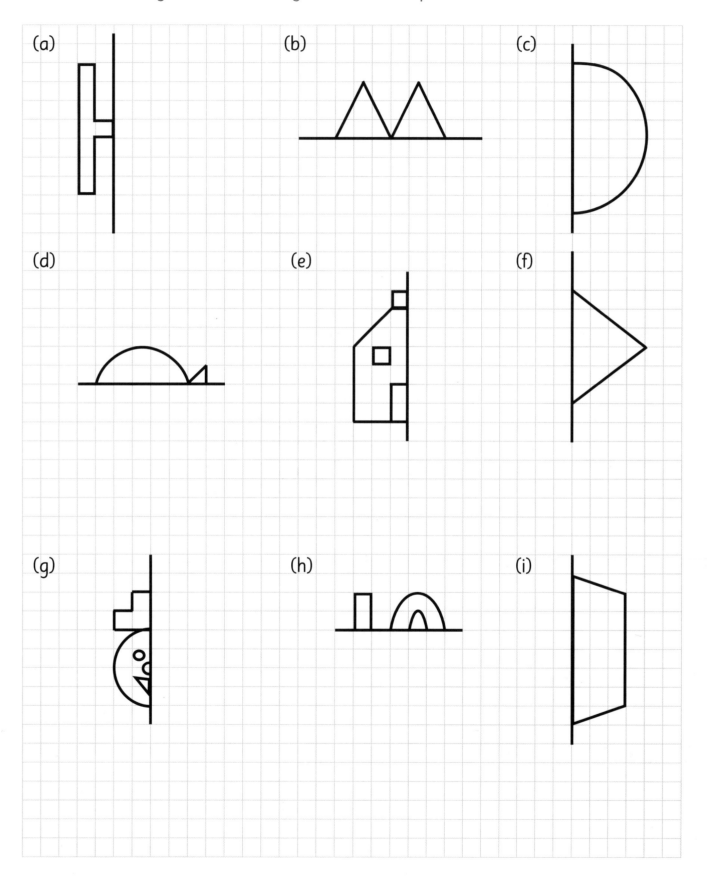

1. (a) 8 x 5 = _____   2.   10   3. 45 ÷ 5 = _____   4. 90 ÷ 10 = _____
                            x 7
                            ___

5. Colour $\frac{6}{10}$ of this shape.

6. What fraction of this shape is coloured?

7. $\frac{6}{10}$ = 0._____   8. 0.7 = ⬜

9.   159   10.   513
        + 238   − 296
        _____   _____

11. Colour 0.4 of these counters.

12. Draw and name a symmetrical 2-D shape.
    (Not a rectangle!)

    _____

13. Draw a shape that is not symmetrical.

14. Ten 5c coins = _____ c   15. Five 10c coins = _____ c

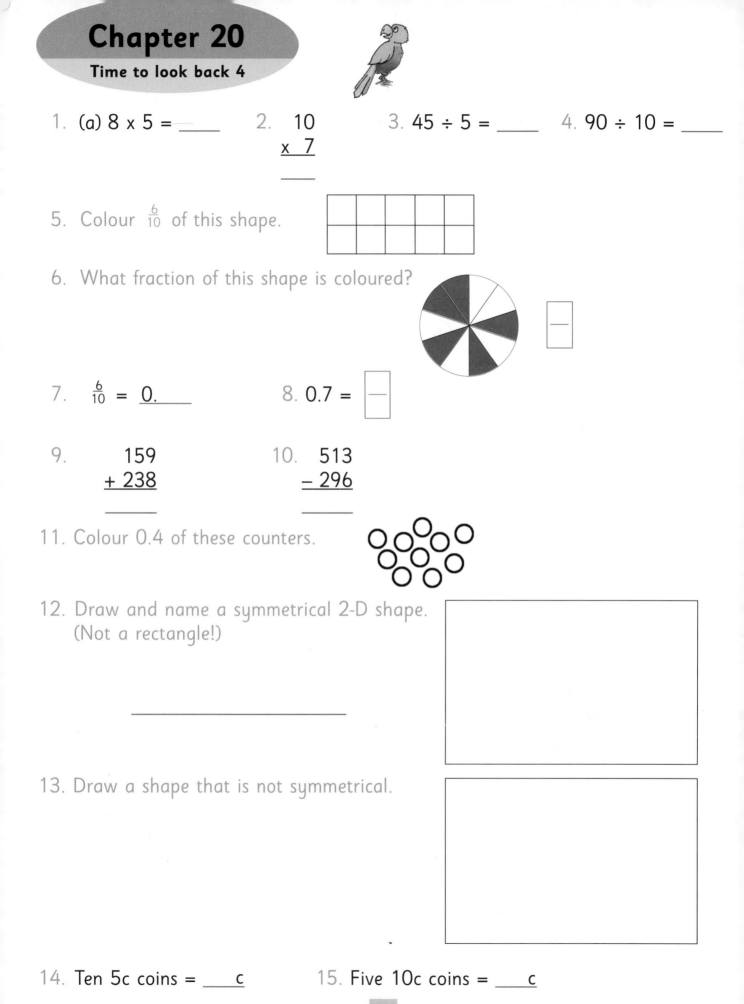

16. During the art lesson 10 children shared
    80 crayons equally. **How many crayons did
    each child get?** _____

17. The 30 children in Zoe's third class sit in 5 equal rows. **If all pupils are
    present, how many children will be in each row?** _____

18. James gave $\frac{1}{8}$ of his 32 football cards to his friend.
    How many cards did he give away? _____

19. James and Zoe counted the symmetrical shapes
    on the basketball court in the yard. **How many
    symmetrical shapes did they find?** _____

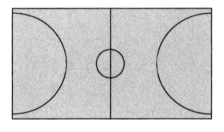

20. After school Zoe's Dad opened a pack of 24 fish fingers
    for tea. He put 0.5 of the fish fingers in the freezer and
    cooked the rest. **How many did he cook?** _____

How well did you do?

Give yourself 1 mark for each question you answered correctly
and then tick the box with your score.

☐	☐	☐	☐
18–20	15–17	10–14	0–9
Excellent	Very good	Good	Keep up the good work

You need:
- to practise multiplication facts 7
- colouring pencils

Multiplying by 7

1. How many books on each shelf? ___
   How many shelves can you see? ___

   7 + 7 + 7 + 7 = 28   **4 x 7 = 28**

2. Colour the multiples of 7 on this part of the hundred square. Now write out the multiples of seven.

1	2	3	4	5	6	7	8	9	10
11	12	13	14	15	16	17	18	19	20
21	22	23	24	25	26	27	28	29	30
31	32	33	34	35	36	37	38	39	40
41	42	43	44	45	46	47	48	49	50
51	52	53	54	55	56	57	58	59	60
61	62	63	64	65	66	67	68	69	70

   ___, ___, ___, ___, ___, ___, ___, ___, ___, ___

3. Try these.
   (a) 7 + 7 + 7 = **3** x **7** = **21**   (b) 7 + 7 + 7 + 7 + 7 + 7 = __ x __ = __
   (c) 7 + 7 + 7 + 7 = __ x __ = __   (d) 7 + 7 = __ x __ = __
   (e) 7 + 7 + 7 + 7 + 7 + 7 + 7 + 7 = __ x __ = __

4. Now try these.
   (a) 9 x 7 = __ + __ + __ + __ + __ + __ + __ + __ + __ = _____
   (b) 10 x 7 = __ + __ + __ + __ + __ + __ + __ + __ + __ + __ = _____

5. How much for
   (a) 2 sweets? __   (b) 3 sweets? __   (c) 7 sweets? __
   (d) 9 sweets? __   (e) 4 sweets? __   (f) 8 sweets? __
   (g) 10 sweets? __   (h) 5 sweets? __   (i) 6 sweets? __

   7c each

6. Try these.
   (a) 5 x 7 = **35**   (b) 7 x 7 = __   (c) 9 x 7 = __   (d) 3 x 7 = __
   (e) 8 x 7 = __   (f) 6 x 7 = __   (g) 2 x 7 = __   (h) 10 x 7 = __

   (8 x 7 = 56) can also be written like this

   ```
     7
   x 8
   ----
    56
   ```

7. (a)   7   (b)   7   (c)   7   (d)   7   (e)   7   (f)   7
       x 3   x 9   x 5   x 10   x 4   x 6
      ____   ____   ____   ____   ____   ____

Problems for you to solve

1. School is closed for 9 weeks during the summer holidays. **How many days is that altogether?** _____

2. A lollipop costs 7c. Kate bought 8 lollipops yesterday. **How much did she pay for them?** _____

3. During the summer holidays Sinéad spent two weeks at a summer camp. She took part in a 7-a-side rounders competition. There were 5 teams altogether. **How many of the children played rounders?** ___

4. Jennifer planted 4 rows of flowers in the garden last week. There were 7 flowers in each row. **How many flowers was that altogether?** _____

5. Tony had 45 World Cup football stickers. He gave 7 to each of his 6 friends. **How many had he left for himself?** _____

Knock Knock...

'Who's there?' ... 'Harry' ... 'Harry Who?'

To find the last line of this joke cross out the numbers that are **not multiples of 7** and the letters above those numbers. Look carefully at the remaining letters and you will find the answer that Harry gave.

H	A	B	R	R	I	Y	B	U	C	P	A	N	D	O	G	P	E	N	T	K	H	E	D	M	O	S	O	R
14	21	17	7	35	3	63	18	35	13	7	14	28	42	49	27	21	63	35	56	41	70	35	42	55	21	29	35	49

Multiplying by 1 and 0

1. How many eggs are in the nest? __

    7 x 1 = 7   or   1 x 7 = 7

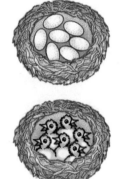

2. How many chicks are in the nest?

    6 x 1 = 6   or   1 x 6 = 6

3. Now try these.

    (a) 5 x 1 = __   (b) 9 x 1 = __   (c) 8 x 1 = __   (d) __ x 1 = 5

    (e) 2 x 1 = __   (f) __ x 8 = 8   (g) __ x 5 = 5   (h) __ x 1 = 10

    (i) 10 x __ = 10   (j) 4 x __ = 4   (k) 6 x __ = 6   (l) 7 x __ = 7

    (m) __ x 1 = 7   (n) 1 x __ = 9   (o) 1 x __ = 2   (p) __ x 1 = 4

4. How many 5c coins in the purse?
    0 x 5 = 0

5. How many 10c coins in the purse?
    0 x 10 = 0

6. How many 2c coins in the purse?
    0 x 2 = 0

7. How many 1c coins in the purse?
    0 x 1 = 0

8. Fill in the blanks.

    (a) 0 x 1 = __   (b) 0 x 4 = __   (c) 0 x 5 = __   (d) 0 x 10 = __

    (e) 0 x 9 = __   (f) 2 x 0 = __   (g) 7 x 0 = __   (h) 10 x 0 = __

    (i) 4 x 0 = __   (j) 8 x 0 = __

9. Fill in the blanks so that all answers = 0

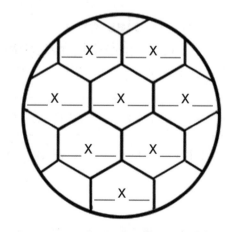

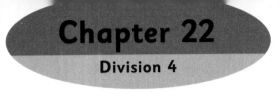

Chapter 22
Division 4

Dividing by 7

1. When the Secret Seven were exploring Brookside Manor, a haunted castle, they discovered an old treasure chest in the dungeon. When they opened it they were very surprised to find a collection of gold coins. There were 63 coins altogether and they shared them equally among themselves.

(a) How many children were there? _____

(b) How many coins did they find? _____

(c) How many coins did each child get? _____

(d) Write it as a division sentence _____ ÷ _____ = _____

2. There are 21 boys and 35 girls in Lisbeg Youth Club. Last summer they took part in the town festival treasure hunt. The leader divided them into groups of 7. How many groups did the Youth Club have in the treasure hunt?

Write an addition sentence first _____ + _____ = _____

Then write a division sentence _____ ÷ _____ = _____

3. Now do these.

(a) 28 ÷ 7 = _____   (b) 42 ÷ 7 = _____   (c) 35 ÷ 7 = _____ (d) 14 ÷ 7 = _____

(e) 49 ÷ 7 = _____   (f) 21 ÷ 7 = _____   (g) 7 ÷ 7 = _____ (h) 70 ÷ 7 = _____

4. There are 7 days in a week. In Italy last year it didn't rain for 49 days. How many weeks is that? ___
Write it as a division sentence ___ ÷ ___ = ___

5.  It takes 7 apples to make an apple crumble. How many crumbles can be made from 35 apples? _____

6. How many 7-a-side teams can be made from 42 players? _____

The 4 ways of division!

Up to now we have used only one symbol (÷) to show division.
There are 4 ways altogether. Look at these examples:

(a) 28 ÷ 7   (b) 7|28   (c) 7|28⎴   (d) $\frac{28}{7}$

Write these in the four different ways.

1. Divide 21 by 7.
    (a) 21 ⎵ 7 = ___   (b) 7 21   (c) 7 21   (d) —

2. Divide 56 by 7.
    (a) 56 ⎵ 7 = ___   (b) 7 56   (c) 7 56   (d) —

3. Divide 42 by 7.
    (a) 42 ⎵ 7 = ___   (b) 7 42   (c) 7 42   (d) —

4. Divide 35 by 7.
    (a) 35 ⎵ 7 = ___   (b) 7 35   (c) 7 35   (d) —

5. Divide 70 by 7.
    (a) 70 ⎵ 7 = ___   (b) 7 70   (c) 7 70   (d) —

6. Divide 49 by 7.
    (a) 49 ⎵ 7 = ___   (b) 7 49   (c) 7 49   (d) —

7. How many weeks in 63 days? _____
    Write the division sentence in the 4 ways.

    (a)   (b)   (c)   (d)

8. A total of 35 cyclists took part in the Dublin to Galway
    stage of a cycle race. There were 7 cyclists in each team.
    How many teams took part? _____
    Write the division sentence in the 4 ways.

    (a)   (b)   (c)   (d)

Linking multiplication and division

 We can write a division sentence and a multiplication sentence about the way these 12 apples are grouped.

3 groups of 4 apples equals 12 apples.

3 x 4 = 12

12 apples divided in groups of 4 is 3 groups.

12 ÷ 4 = 3

We can write a different multiplication sentence and a different division sentence about these 12 apples.

4 groups of 3 apples equals 12 apples.

4 x 3 = 12

12 apples divided in groups of 3 is 4 groups.

12 ÷ 3 = 4

 1.

Look at these 15 jam tarts. With your pencil divide them in 3 groups. Now write a multiplication sentence and a division sentence about the tarts.

Now look at the same 15 jam tarts again. With your pencil divide them in 5 groups. Now write a multiplication sentence and a division sentence about the tarts.

___ x ___ = ___   ___ ÷ ___ = ___   ___ x ___ = ___   ___ ÷ ___ = ___

2. Get 20 counters or lollipop sticks and divide them into groups. You could use straws to separate the groups from each other.
   How many division and multiplication sentences can you write? ___

3. Write multiplication and division sentences using these groups of numbers.

2 6 12	3 6 18	5 6 30	6 9 54

___ x ___ = ___   ___ x ___ = ___   ___ x ___ = ___   ___ x ___ = ___

___ x ___ = ___   ___ x ___ = ___   ___ x ___ = ___   ___ x ___ = ___

___ ÷ ___ = ___   ___ ÷ ___ = ___   ___ ÷ ___ = ___   ___ ÷ ___ = ___

___ ÷ ___ = ___   ___ ÷ ___ = ___   ___ ÷ ___ = ___   ___ ÷ ___ = ___

Remainders

Divide these 13 oranges into groups of 4.

There are 3 groups of 4 oranges and 1 orange left over. 13 ÷ 4 = 3 remainder 1.

From now on we will write it like this: 4 ⌊13
                                          ‾‾‾‾
                                          3 r 1

1. Divide these 14 pencils into groups of 3.

   Fill in the missing numbers:
   There are _____ groups of _____ pencils with _____ pencils left over.
   Now write it as a division sentence. 3 ⌊___
                                          ___ r ___

2. Get 17 counters or lollipops and divide them into groups of 5.
   How many groups did you get? _____
   How many were left over? _____
   Now write it as a division sentence. ___ ⌊___
                                          ___ r ___

3. Now do these.

   (a) 9⌊13   (b) 2⌊19   (c) 3⌊23   (d) 3⌊29   (e) 4⌊23   (f) 4⌊33
      ‾‾‾‾   ‾‾‾‾   ‾‾‾‾   ‾‾‾‾   ‾‾‾‾   ‾‾‾‾

   (g) 5⌊17   (h) 5⌊31   (i) 6⌊37   (j) 7⌊40   (k) 8⌊57   (l) 9⌊48
      ‾‾‾‾   ‾‾‾‾   ‾‾‾‾   ‾‾‾‾   ‾‾‾‾   ‾‾‾‾

4. How many bundles of 5 books can I make from 28 books and how many will be left over? _____ , _____

5.  Gavin had 50c. He went to the shops and bought sweets at 8c each. How many sweets could he buy with the money and how much change should he get back from the shopkeeper? _____ , _____

6. A class of 37 children was divided into 7-a-side teams. How many teams were made and how many children were left without getting on a team?

   _____ , _____

You need:
- colouring pencils
- to revise concept of $\frac{1}{2}$, $\frac{1}{4}$, $\frac{1}{8}$ and $\frac{1}{10}$

The artist has not finished this picture and you can help her out.

1. Only half of the trees have been put in the picture.
   How many trees can you see? ___
   $\frac{1}{2}$ = **4**   Full amount ($\frac{2}{2}$) = 2 x **4** = ___ trees.

2. One quarter of the children appear in the picture.
   How many children can you see? ___
   $\frac{1}{4}$ = ___   Full amount ($\frac{4}{4}$) = 4 x ___ = ___ children.

3. Look at the pond. Only one eighth of the ducks have been drawn.
   How many ducks can you see? ___
   $\frac{1}{8}$ = ___   Full amount ($\frac{8}{8}$) = 8 x ___ = ___ ducks.

4. One tenth of the flowers have been put into the flower bed.
   How many flowers has the artist drawn? ___
   $\frac{1}{10}$ = ___   Full amount ($\frac{10}{10}$) = 10 x ___ = ___ flowers.

5. Now put in the correct number of trees, children, ducks and flowers to finish the picture. Finish colouring the picture.

Problems for you to solve

1. There are 24 children in this third class.
   (a) Half the class walk to school.
   How many children walk to school? _____
   (b) One quarter of the children take the bus to school. How many children travel by bus? _____
   (c) One eighth of the class cycle to school.
   How many children cycle to school? _____

2.  Ms Ryan, the third class teacher, divided her class into 4 groups for P.E. Here she is with one group.
   (a) How many children are there in Ms Ryan's class? _____
   (b) One tenth of the children offered to tidy up after the lesson. How many children offered to tidy up? _____

3. One eighth of the teachers in this school wear glasses. Here they are.
   How many teachers work in the school? _____

4.  Mr Nolan, the caretaker, has washed 8 windows so far. That is one quarter of the total number of windows in the school. How many windows are in the school? _____

5. (a) $\frac{1}{4}$ of a number is 6. The number is _____   (e) $\frac{1}{4}$ of _____ is 9.

   (b) $\frac{1}{2}$ of a number is 10. The number is. _____   (f) $\frac{1}{2}$ of _____ is 8.

   (c) $\frac{1}{10}$ of a number is 8. The number is _____   (g) $\frac{1}{10}$ of _____ is 9.

   (d) $\frac{1}{8}$ of a number is 3. The number is. _____   (h) $\frac{1}{8}$ of _____ is 6.

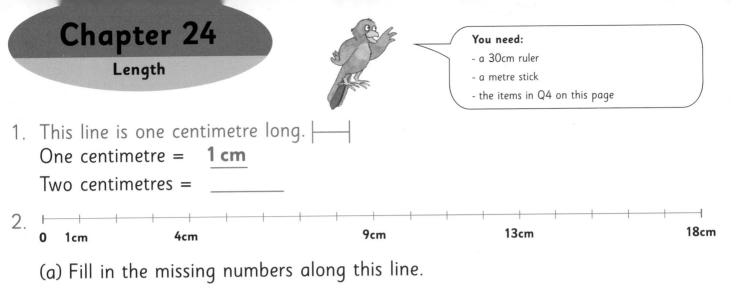

You need:
- a 30cm ruler
- a metre stick
- the items in Q4 on this page

1. This line is one centimetre long. ⊢—⊣
   One centimetre = __1 cm__
   Two centimetres = _____

2.

| 0 | 1cm | | 4cm | | | 9cm | | | 13cm | | | | 18cm |

   (a) Fill in the missing numbers along this line.

   (b) Use your ruler to measure the line.

   (c) This line is _____ cm long.

3. Look at these pictures.

   (a) Colour the things you think are shorter than 15cm in red.
   (b) Colour the things you think are longer than 15cm in blue.

4. Estimate the lengths of these things and then measure each one in centimetres. Record your results in the grid.

	Estimate	Measure	Difference
my shoe	____ cm	____ cm	____ cm
my arm	____ cm	____ cm	____ cm
a pencil	____ cm	____ cm	____ cm
pencil case	____ cm	____ cm	____ cm
maths book	____ cm	____ cm	____ cm
roll book	____ cm	____ cm	____ cm

Using metres

1. We use metres to measure longer objects.
   Here is a picture of a metre stick.

   (a) Fill in the missing numbers on the metre stick.

   (b) 1 metre = ____ cm.

   (c) 1 metre may be written like this: **1m**

2. More or less than 1 metre?

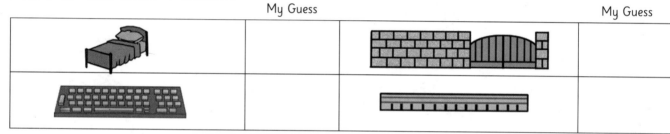

	My Guess		My Guess

   This is Sean with his dad. Dad is 179 cm in height.
   179cm = 100cm + 79cm = 1m 79cm
   Sean is 127 cm in height.
   127cm = 100cm + 27cm = 1m 27cm.

3. Now try these.

   (a) 160cm = ____ m ____ cm   (b) 1m 56cm = ____ cm

   (c) 196cm = ____ m ____ cm   (d) 1m 20cm = ____ cm

   (e) 102cm = ____ m ____ cm   (f) 1m 16cm = ____ cm

   (g) 145cm = ____ m ____ cm   (h) 1m 99cm = ____ cm

   (i) 210cm = ____ m ____ cm   (j) 2m 17cm = ____ cm

4. Use a metre stick to measure the following objects and record your results.

	Estimate	Measure	✓ Good Estimate ✗ Poor Estimate
height of door	____ m ____ cm	____ m ____ cm	
teacher's desk	____ m ____ cm	____ m ____ cm	
length of classroom	____ m ____ cm	____ m ____ cm	

Addition and subtraction of metres and centimetres

Joey is back! He has hopped twice already. Each time he hopped he travelled 1m 56cm! How far has he travelled after 2 hops? _____

(1) Add the centimetres.
   56cm + 56cm = 112cm = 100cm + 12cm = 1m 12cm

	m	cm
	1	5 6
+	1₁	5₁6
Ans:	3	1 2

(2) Put 12cm in the centimetre place and bring over 1 metre to the metres place.
(3) Add the metres. 1m + 1m + 1m = 3m

1. Now try these.

(a)
m	cm
1	29
+ 1	86

(b)
m	cm
1	64
+ 1	56

(c)
m	cm
1	76
+ 1	62

(d)
m	cm
1	38
+ 1	93

(e)
m	cm
1	57
+ 1	88

(f)
m	cm
1	96
+ 1	34

(g)
m	cm
1	60
+ 1	40

(h)
m	cm
1	72
+ 1	89

Joey had travelled 4m 16cm up this hill when he slipped and fell back 1m 88cm. Poor Joey! How far had he travelled now?

(1) You cannot take 88cm from 16cm.
   Bring over 1 metre = 100cm.
   Change 4m to 3m. Subtract the cm.
(2) Subtract the metres.
   3m – 1m = 2m

	m	cm
	³4	¹⁰1̶6
–	1	88
Ans:	2	28

2. Now try these.

(a)
m	cm
3	16
– 1	57

(b)
m	cm
4	38
– 1	86

(c)
m	cm
3	17
– 1	28

(d)
m	cm
2	60
– 1	80

3. (a) 3m 26cm – 1m 35cm = _____   (b) 3m 19cm – 1m 69cm = _____

   (c) 5m 26cm – 2m 86cm = _____   (d) 6m 3cm – 1m 74cm = _____

Playing in the park

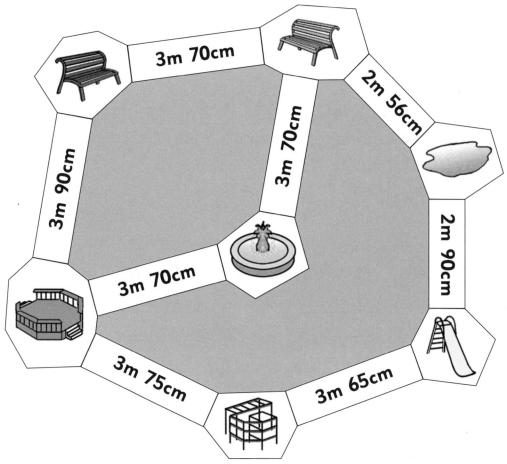

Look at the length of the paths in the park to help you to find the answers.

1. The longest path is _____m _____cm in length.

2. The shortest path is _____m _____cm in length.

3. How far is it from the climbing frame to the bandstand and on to the fountain? _____m _____cm

4. Áine ran from the red bench to the green bench and on to the fountain. How far did she run? _____m _____cm

5. Mary ran from the slide to the pond and on to the green bench. How far did she run?_____m _____cm

6. _____ ran _____m _____cm farther than _____.

7. Sinéad was at the green bench. She walked exactly 7m 40cm. Where is she now? _____

You need:
- euro coins   - to explain currency
- a euro sign card for each pupil
- a decimal point card for each pupil
- 2 sets of 0 – 9 numerals for each group of 4

There are 8 coins in the euro currency. The coin with the lowest value is 1c. The coin with the highest value is €2.

There are 100 cent in €1. One euro can also be written as €1.00.

50c can also be written as €0.50.

136c is written as €1.36.

We never use the cent sign (c) and the euro sign (€) together.

1. Use as few coins as possible to buy these items. The first one is done for you.

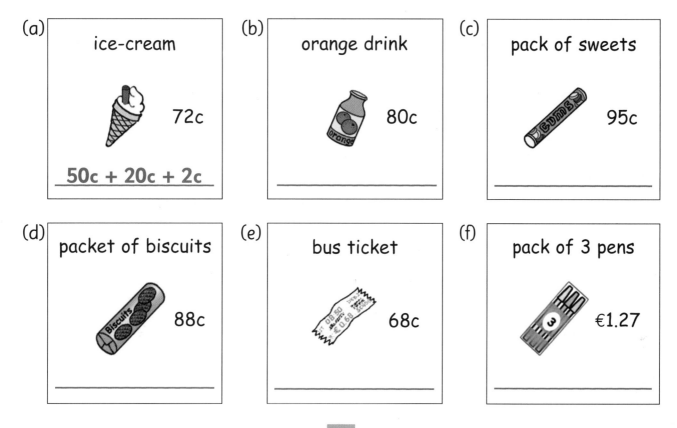

(a)
ice-cream

72c

50c + 20c + 2c

(b)
orange drink

80c

_____

(c)
pack of sweets

95c

_____

(d)
packet of biscuits

88c

_____

(e)
bus ticket

68c

_____

(f)
pack of 3 pens

€1.27

_____

Euro and cent

1. How much money is in each of these purses?

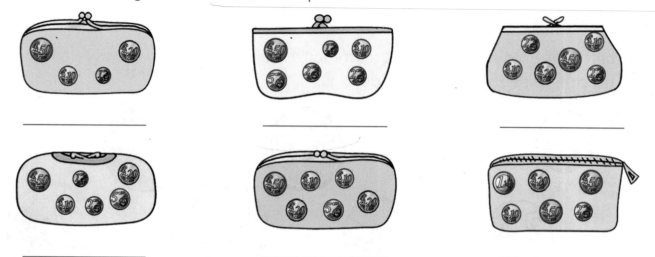

_____ _____ _____

_____ _____ _____

2. Use as few coins as possible to make the following amounts.

(a) 17c = **10c + 5c + 2c**   (b) 26c = _____

(c) 47c = _____   (d) 59c = _____

(e) 84c = _____   (f) 95c = _____

(g) €1.25 = _____   (h) €1.62 = _____

(i) €2.48 = _____   (j) €4.30 = _____

3. Write these amounts in cent.
(a) €1.20 = **120c**   (b) €1.40 = ____   (c) €1.75 = ____

(d) €1.96 = ____   (e) €2.80 = ____   (f) €2.08 = ____

(g) €3.10 = ____   (h) €3.30 = ____   (i) €4.03 = ____

(j) €5.80 = ____   (k) €6.90 = ____   (l) €7.09 = ____

4. Write these amounts using the € sign.

(a) 43c = **€0.43**   (b) 68c = ____   (c) 98c = ____

(d) 120c = ____   (e) 165c = ____   (f) 180c = ____

(g) 208c = ____   (h) 310c = ____   (i) 9c = ____

Addition and subtraction

Martha bought a pencil case for €1.55 and a plastic ruler for 80c.
How much did she pay altogether?

€1.55
+ €0.80
―――――
€2.35

Martha paid €2.35 altogether for the pencil case and the ruler.

1. Try these.

(a)   €1.95
     + €2.32
     ―――――

(b)   €1.87
     + €0.50
     ―――――

(c)   €2.48
     + €1.51
     ―――――

(d)   €2.47
     + €0.90
     ―――――

(e)   €2.43
     + €1.48
     ―――――

(f)   €3.27
     + €1.69
     ―――――

(g)   €5.24
     + €2.69
     ―――――

(h)   €4.72
     + €2.19
     ―――――

2. These are addition questions also but they are written in a different way.
   Write them down properly in the spaces below and then add them up.

(a) 72c + €1.64 + €2.40
(b) €3.67 + 72c + €1.08
(c) 84c + 9c + €1.14
(d) €1.50 + 19c + 84c
(e) 6c + €3.47 + 95c
(f) €2.05 + 110c + 18c

(a) € .
    € .
    € .
    ―――
    € .

(b) € .
    € .
    € .
    ―――
    € .

(c) € .
    € .
    € .
    ―――
    € .

(d) € .
    € .
    € .
    ―――
    € .

(e) € .
    € .
    € .
    ―――
    € .

(f) € .
    € .
    € .
    ―――
    € .

George had €2.56 but he bought a football magazine for €1.69.
How much has he left?

€2.56
− €1.69
―――――
€0.87

He has 87c left.

3. Try these.

(a)   €2.64
     − €1.39
     ―――――

(b)   €2.72
     − €1.46
     ―――――

(c)   €3.84
     − €1.65
     ―――――

(d)   €4.96
     − €2.47
     ―――――

(e)   €5.82
     − €3.65
     ―――――

(f)   €4.69
     − €2.84
     ―――――

(g)   €5.28
     − €2.76
     ―――――

(h)   €3.39
     − €1.86
     ―――――

(i)   €5.19
     − €2.78
     ―――――

(j)   €4.00
     − €1.76
     ―――――

School Sale of Work

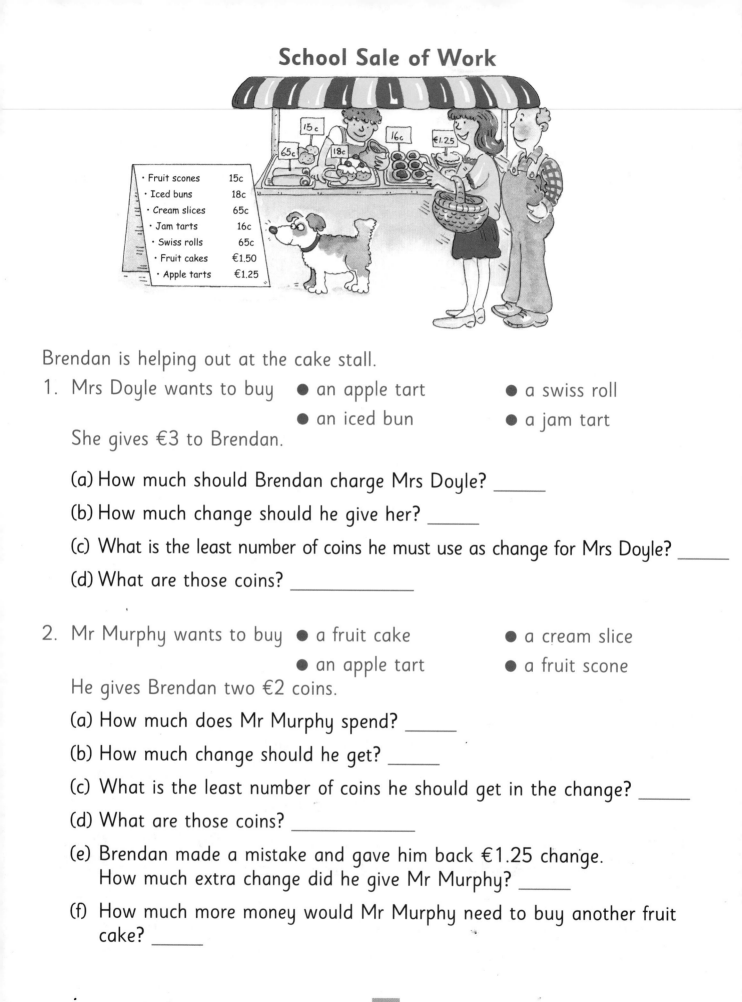

Brendan is helping out at the cake stall.

1. Mrs Doyle wants to buy   ● an apple tart   ● a swiss roll

                                ● an iced bun   ● a jam tart

    She gives €3 to Brendan.

    (a) How much should Brendan charge Mrs Doyle? _____

    (b) How much change should he give her? _____

    (c) What is the least number of coins he must use as change for Mrs Doyle? _____

    (d) What are those coins? _____

2. Mr Murphy wants to buy   ● a fruit cake   ● a cream slice

                              ● an apple tart   ● a fruit scone

    He gives Brendan two €2 coins.

    (a) How much does Mr Murphy spend? _____

    (b) How much change should he get? _____

    (c) What is the least number of coins he should get in the change? _____

    (d) What are those coins? _____

    (e) Brendan made a mistake and gave him back €1.25 change.
        How much extra change did he give Mr Murphy? _____

    (f) How much more money would Mr Murphy need to buy another fruit cake? _____

Fun with money

1. The amounts of money that were added or subtracted in these questions have fallen down. Can you put them back in the correct places?

Addition

(a)

€__ .__ __
+€__ .__ __
―――――
€13 . 1 4

(b)

€__ .__ __
+€__ .__ __
―――――
€12 . 3 6

(c)

€__ .__ __
+€__ .__ __
―――――
€13 . 7 5

(d)

€__ .__ __
+€__ .__ __
―――――
€12 . 8 4

€5.47   €6.97   €6.58   €6.78   €5.99   €6.56   €6.85   €6.89

Subtraction

(e)

€__.__ __
−€__.__ __
―――――
€ 2 . 7 7

(f)

€__.__ __
−€__.__ __
―――――
€ 2 . 7 5

(g)

€__.__ __
−€__.__ __
―――――
€ 2 . 7 9

(h)

€__.__ __
−€__.__ __
―――――
€ 2 . 7 4

€9.56   €7.45   €8.26   €9.72   €10.19   €5.47   €6.95   €12.31

A card game for up to four players

(a) Each player needs a euro sign **€** card and a decimal point card **.** . The dealer has two sets of numeral cards 0–9 which she shuffles. She gives each player four numeral cards. Each player then makes the biggest amount of money possible. So if you got **2 7 0 1** you could make **€ 7 2 . 1 0**. You must have two numbers before and after the decimal point. The person who makes the largest amount wins!

(b) You could change the rules and decide that the person who makes the smallest amount wins.

(c) If the dealer gives 5 cards to each player, then each player must have three numbers before the decimal point and two numbers after the decimal point.

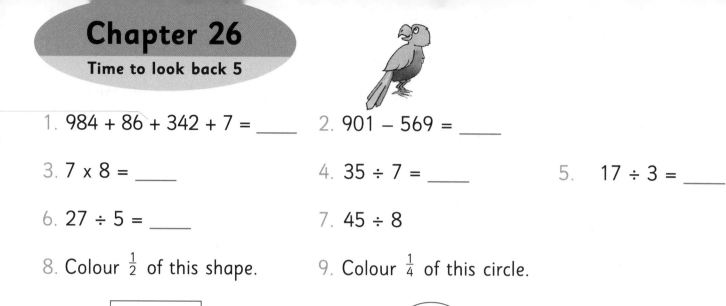

1. 984 + 86 + 342 + 7 = _____   2. 901 – 569 = _____

3. 7 x 8 = _____   4. 35 ÷ 7 = _____   5.   17 ÷ 3 = _____

6. 27 ÷ 5 = _____   7. 45 ÷ 8

8. Colour $\frac{1}{2}$ of this shape.   9. Colour $\frac{1}{4}$ of this circle.

10. Colour in $\frac{1}{8}$ of this stone wall.

11. m   cm   12. m   cm   13.   14. €4.53 – €2.67 = _____
     4   26   1   64   €3.48
    +3   84   – 1   56   – €2.57
    _____   _____   _____

15. Martin's big brother wanted to rent a video.
    The cost of renting a video for one night
    was €4.50 but he only had €1.85.
    How much more did he need? _____

16.    Gemma is 1m 28cm and her Dad is 40cm taller.
    How tall is her Dad? _____

17. There are 8 girls in third class in Ballybeg School. That's $\frac{1}{4}$ of the whole class. **How many children altogether in the class?** _____

18.  There were 63 children in St Michael's Youth Club. The leader divided them into groups of 7. **How many groups were there?** _____

19. The third class children in Bigbrook School line up in 4 groups when they are coming in from the playground. There are 7 in each group. **How many children altogether in the class?** _____

20.  Farmer Green's hens laid 47 eggs last Monday. He put them into boxes of 6. **How many eggs was he short of to fill the last box?** _____

How well did you do?

Give yourself 1 mark for each question you answered correctly and then tick the box with your score.

☐   ☐   ☐   ☐

18–20	15–17	10–14	0–9
Excellent	Very good	Good	Keep up the good work

Chapter 27
Time 1

You need:
- digital and analogue clocks and watches

1. (a) What time is shown on this clock? ____ o'clock
   (b) What time will the clock show one hour later? ____ o'clock
   The clock face is divided into 4 equal parts.
   Each part is $\boxed{\frac{-}{4}}$ of an hour.

2. One hour = 60 minutes
   15 mins + 15 mins + 15 mins + 15 mins = ____ minutes

3. (a) What time is it? $\boxed{\frac{-}{}}$ past ____
   (b) How many minutes past nine? ____ minutes.

4. (a) What time is it? $\boxed{\frac{-}{}}$ past ____
   (b) How many quarters past nine? ____ $\boxed{\frac{-}{4}} = \boxed{\frac{-}{2}}$
   (c) How many minutes past nine? **15** + ____ = ____ minutes
   (d) How many minutes to go before 10 o'clock? ____ minutes

5. (a) What time is it now? $\boxed{\frac{-}{}}$ to ____
   (b) How many quarters past nine? $\boxed{\frac{-}{4}}$
   (c) How many minutes past nine? 15 + ____ + **15** = ____
   (d) How many minutes before 10 o'clock? ____ minutes

6. (a) It is ____ o'clock.
   (b) How many quarters have passed since 9 o'clock? $\boxed{\frac{-}{}}$
   (c) How many minutes have passed since 9 o'clock? ____
   15 + ____ + ____ + ____ = ____ minutes = ____ hour.

7. (a) $\frac{1}{4}$ of an hour = ____ minutes.   (b) $\frac{2}{4}$ or $\frac{1}{2}$ an hour = ____ minutes.
   (c) $\frac{3}{4}$ of an hour = ____ minutes.   (d) $\frac{4}{4}$ or 1 hour = ____ minutes.

5-minute intervals

1. 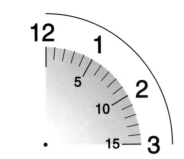 Here is a quarter of a clock face.
$\frac{1}{4}$ of an hour = 15 minutes.
Can you count 15 notches on the clock face?
The minute hand takes 5 minutes to travel from
12 to 1. Count the notches between
12 and 1 on the clock face.

(a) The minute hand travels from 12 to 2 in _____ mins.
(b) The minute hand travels from 12 to 3 in _____ mins.

2. Write the time under each clock. The first one is done for you.

(a) **5** minutes past **10**   (b) __ minutes past __   (c) __ minutes past __

or ⬚ past 10

3. Fill in the blanks.

0, 5, 10, ____, ____, 25, ____, ____, ____, 45, ____, ____, 60

4. (a) 30 + __ = 60   (b) 35 + __ = 60   (c) 10 + __ = 60   (d) 15 + __ = 60

5. Can you fill in the number of minutes inside this clock face starting at 5. Some have already been done for you.

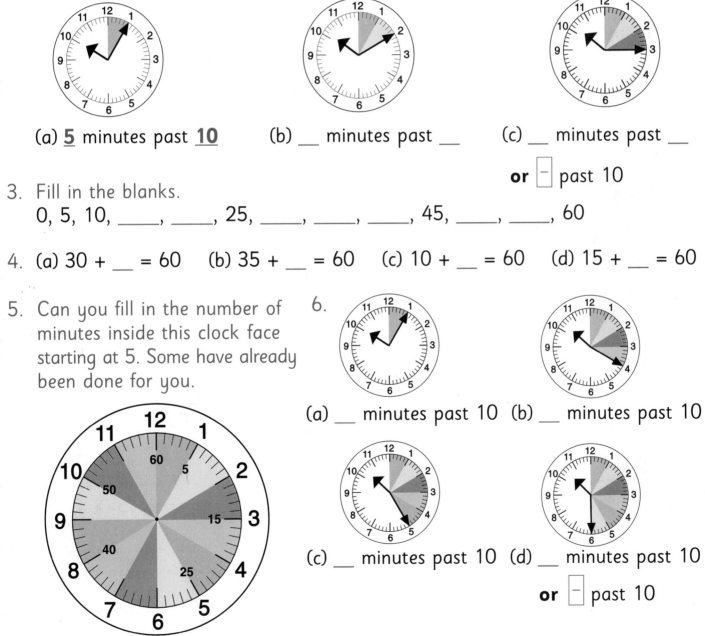

6.

(a) __ minutes past 10   (b) __ minutes past 10

(c) __ minutes past 10   (d) __ minutes past 10

or ⬚ past 10

Digital and analogue

1. Susan and Kate agreed to meet at the school gate at $\frac{1}{2}$ past 3.
   Both girls arrived a little early. Look at the watches. Susan's watch
   has two hands but Kate's is different. Kate has a digital watch.

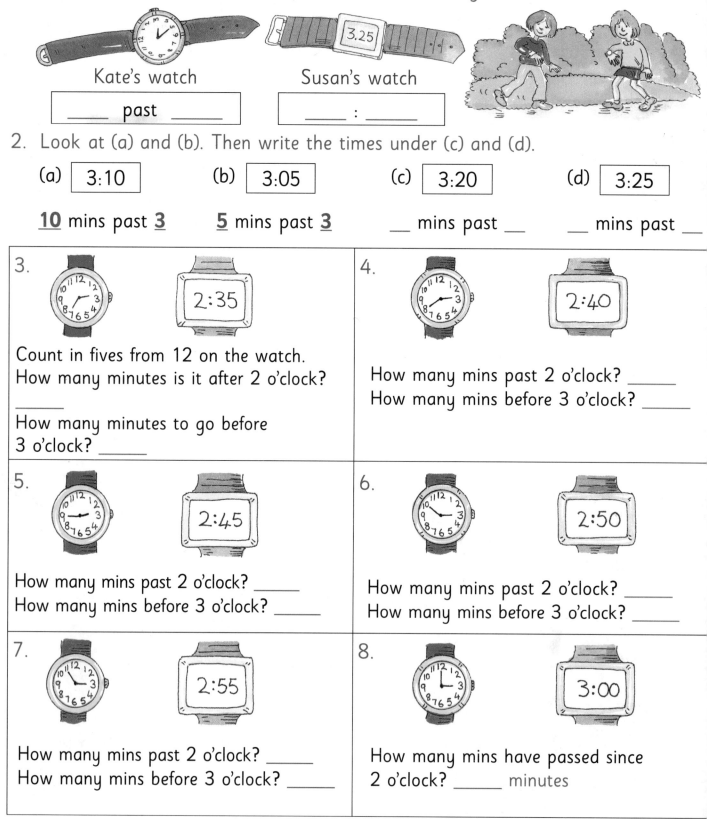

   Kate's watch

   | _____ past _____ |

   Susan's watch

   | _____ : _____ |

2. Look at (a) and (b). Then write the times under (c) and (d).

   (a) | 3:10 | (b) | 3:05 | (c) | 3:20 | (d) | 3:25 |

   10 mins past **3**   **5** mins past **3**   __ mins past __   __ mins past __

3. Count in fives from 12 on the watch.
   How many minutes is it after 2 o'clock?
   _____
   How many minutes to go before
   3 o'clock? _____

   2:35

4. How many mins past 2 o'clock? _____
   How many mins before 3 o'clock? _____

   2:40

5. How many mins past 2 o'clock? _____
   How many mins before 3 o'clock? _____

   2:45

6. How many mins past 2 o'clock? _____
   How many mins before 3 o'clock? _____

   2:50

7. How many mins past 2 o'clock? _____
   How many mins before 3 o'clock? _____

   2:55

8. How many mins have passed since
   2 o'clock? _____ minutes

   3:00

A busy day

Here are some of the things Tom did last Saturday.
Fill in the times on the clocks.

Tom got up at ten minutes past nine.

He helped Dad to wash the dog at twenty minutes past ten.

Tom and Claire went to the shops at half past eleven.

The family had lunch at a quarter to one.

Here is Tom playing a computer game at three o'clock.

Tom's friend Paul called at five to four.

Claire and Tom cleared up after dinner at ten to seven.

Tom watched his favourite TV programme at twenty-five past eight.

The programme lasted 45 minutes.
What time did it finish? _____

9·10

Matching pairs

Match a box from the left side of this page with a box on the right by putting numbers in the empty number boxes. The first one is done for you.

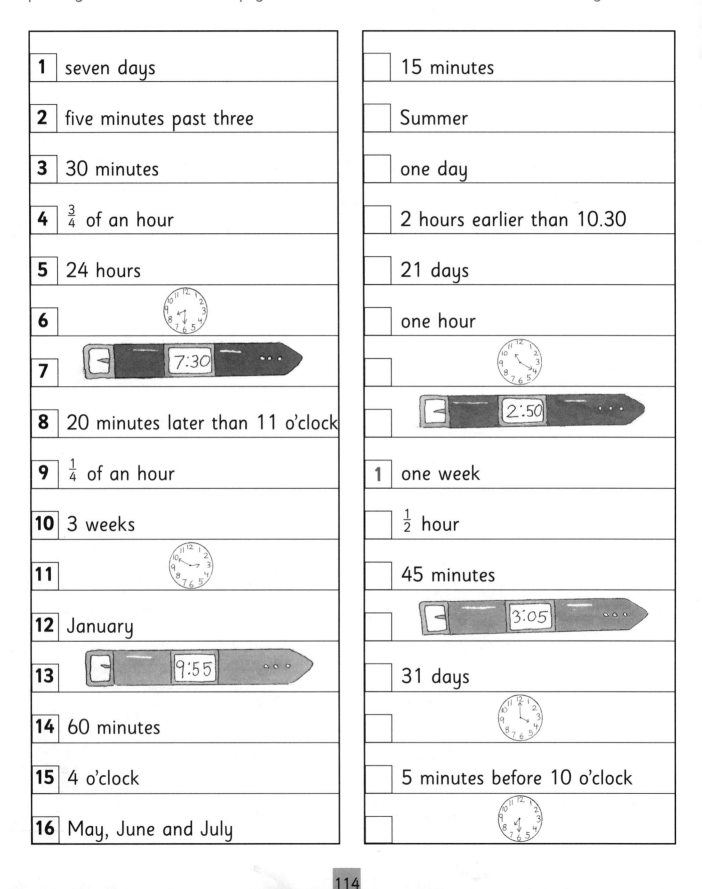

1 seven days		15 minutes
2 five minutes past three		Summer
3 30 minutes		one day
4 $\frac{3}{4}$ of an hour		2 hours earlier than 10.30
5 24 hours		21 days
6		one hour
7 7:30		2:50
8 20 minutes later than 11 o'clock		
9 $\frac{1}{4}$ of an hour	**1** one week
10 3 weeks		$\frac{1}{2}$ hour
11		45 minutes
12 January		3:05
13 9:55		31 days
14 60 minutes		
15 4 o'clock		5 minutes before 10 o'clock
16 May, June and July		

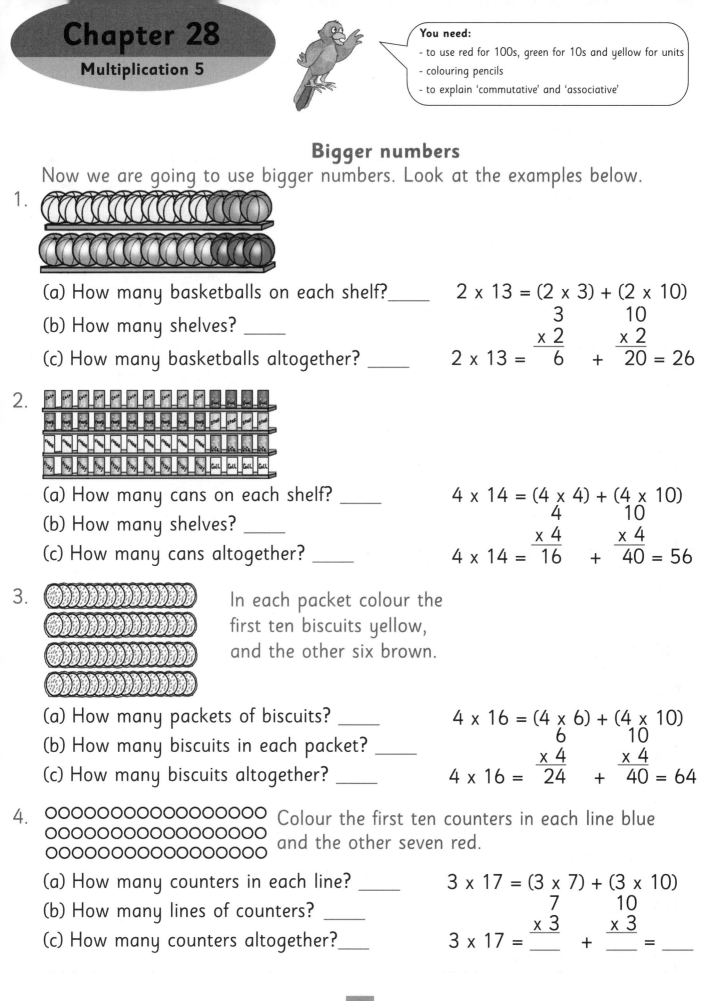

You need:
- to use red for 100s, green for 10s and yellow for units
- colouring pencils
- to explain 'commutative' and 'associative'

Bigger numbers

Now we are going to use bigger numbers. Look at the examples below.

1.

(a) How many basketballs on each shelf?_____ $2 \times 13 = (2 \times 3) + (2 \times 10)$

(b) How many shelves? _____

(c) How many basketballs altogether? _____ $2 \times 13 = \begin{array}{c} 3 \\ \times 2 \\ \hline 6 \end{array} + \begin{array}{c} 10 \\ \times 2 \\ \hline 20 \end{array} = 26$

2.

(a) How many cans on each shelf? _____ $4 \times 14 = (4 \times 4) + (4 \times 10)$

(b) How many shelves? _____

(c) How many cans altogether? _____ $4 \times 14 = \begin{array}{c} 4 \\ \times 4 \\ \hline 16 \end{array} + \begin{array}{c} 10 \\ \times 4 \\ \hline 40 \end{array} = 56$

3.   In each packet colour the first ten biscuits yellow, and the other six brown.

(a) How many packets of biscuits? _____ $4 \times 16 = (4 \times 6) + (4 \times 10)$

(b) How many biscuits in each packet? _____

(c) How many biscuits altogether? _____ $4 \times 16 = \begin{array}{c} 6 \\ \times 4 \\ \hline 24 \end{array} + \begin{array}{c} 10 \\ \times 4 \\ \hline 40 \end{array} = 64$

4.   Colour the first ten counters in each line blue and the other seven red.

(a) How many counters in each line? _____ $3 \times 17 = (3 \times 7) + (3 \times 10)$

(b) How many lines of counters? _____

(c) How many counters altogether?___ $3 \times 17 = \begin{array}{c} 7 \\ \times 3 \\ \hline \end{array} + \begin{array}{c} 10 \\ \times 3 \\ \hline \end{array} = $

A quicker way

Now here is a quicker way to get your answer.

1. There are twelve months in one year. How many months in 2 years? 2 x 12

t	u
1	2
x	2
	4

(a) 2 x 2 units = 4. Put 4 in the units place on the answer line.

t	u
1	2
x	2
2	4

(b) 2 x 1 ten = 2 tens. Put 2 in the tens place on the answer line.

Ans: 2 x 12 = 24

2. Each packet contains 26 sweets. How many sweets altogether? 2 x 26

t	u
2	6
x	2
	2

(a) 2 x 6 = 12 Put 2 in the units place on the answer line.

t	u
2	6
x 1	2
	2

(b) Bring the one ten over to the tens place and put it above the line.

t	u
2	6
x 1	2
5	2

(c) 2 x 2 tens = 4 tens
4 tens + 1 ten = 5 tens
Put 5 in the tens place on the answer line.

Ans: 2 x 26 = 52

3. Now try these.

(a)
t	u
1	3
x ☐	3

(b)
t	u
1	4
x ☐	2

(c)
t	u
1	3
x ☐	2

(d)
t	u
1	2
x ☐	4

(e)
t	u
1	6
x ☐	2

(f)
t	u
1	5
x ☐	2

(g)
t	u
1	4
x ☐	3

(h)
t	u
1	3
x ☐	5

(i)
t	u
1	6
x ☐	3

(j)
t	u
2	5
x ☐	3

(k)
t	u
2	7
x ☐	2

(l)
t	u
2	4
x ☐	4

Even bigger numbers

1. The teacher bought 5 packets of markers for art classes. Each packet contained 24 markers. How many markers altogether?
5 x 24

t	u
2	4
x	5
	0

(a) 5 x 4 = 20
Put 0 in the units place on the answer line.

t	u
2	4
x 2	5
	0

(b) Bring the two tens over to the tens place and put it above the line.

h	t	u
	2	4
x	2	5
1	2	0

(c) 5 x 2 tens = 10 tens
10 tens + 2 tens from above the line = 12 tens
Put the 2 in the tens place and the 1 in the hundreds place.

Ans: 5 x 24 = 120

2. There were 4 packs of copybooks in the school shop. Each pack contained 48 copybooks. How many copybooks altogether?
4 x 48

t	u
4	8
x	4
	2

(a) 4 x 8 = 32
Put the 2 in the units place on the answer line.

t	u
4	8
x 3	4
	2

(b) Bring over the three tens and put 3 above the line.

h	t	u
	4	8
x	3	4
1	9	2

(c) 4 x 4 tens = 16 tens
16 tens + 3 tens from the line = 19 tens.
Put the 9 in the tens place and the 1 in the hundreds place.

Ans: 4 x 48 = 192

3. Now try these.

h	t	u
	3	6
x	□	5

h	t	u
	4	9
x	□	4

h	t	u
	5	7
x	□	5

h	t	u
	6	8
x	□	6

4.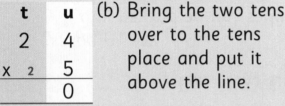

(a) This bus has 54 seats. How many children are there if 4 buses are full?

h	t	u
	5	4
x	□	4

(b) The school bus does 10 trips in a week. How many passengers travel in a week if the bus is full on every trip?

h	t	u
x	□	

A magical machine

1. The workers in the toy factory use this machine to make 29 skipping ropes every day. How many ropes are made in (a) 5 days? _____ (b) 10 days? _____

2. The skipping ropes are packed into boxes each containing 60 ropes to be delivered to toy shops. How many ropes can be packed into
   (a) 6 boxes? _____   (b) 8 boxes? _____   (c) 10 boxes? _____

3. The machine can also make 38 teddy bears every day. How many bears are made in
   (a) 3 days? _____   (b) 5 days? _____   (c) 7 days? _____

4. The teddy bears are packed into boxes each containing 24 bears. One toy shop ordered 4 boxes of teddy bears. How many bears were delivered to the toy shop? _____

5. The workers used the machine to produce 33 basketballs on Monday, 33 on Tuesday and 31 basketballs each day on Wednesday, Thursday and Friday. How many basketballs were made during the five days? _____

Dominoes!

Work out the answers to the sums on these dominoes and then put them in the correct place below.

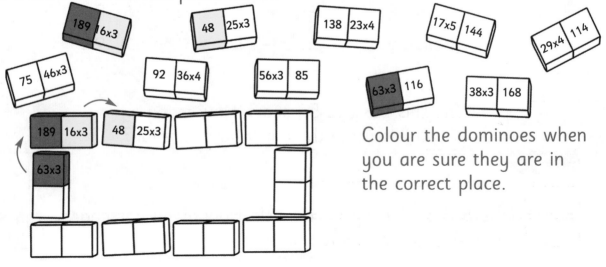

Colour the dominoes when you are sure they are in the correct place.

118

Multiplication

1. How many squares of chocolate in each bar? _____

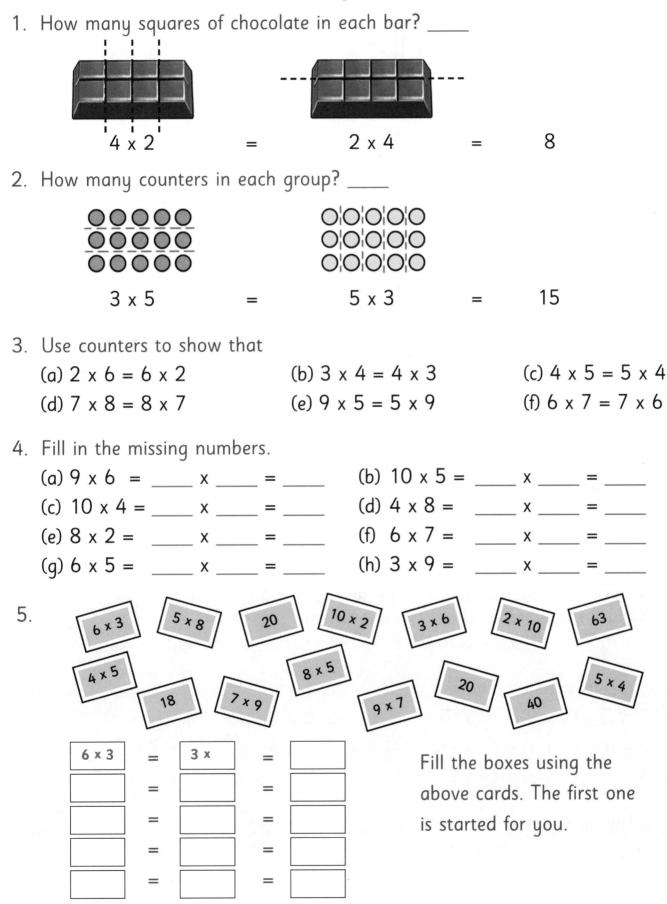

     4 x 2   =   2 x 4   =   8

2. How many counters in each group? _____

     3 x 5   =   5 x 3   =   15

3. Use counters to show that

   (a) 2 x 6 = 6 x 2   (b) 3 x 4 = 4 x 3   (c) 4 x 5 = 5 x 4
   (d) 7 x 8 = 8 x 7   (e) 9 x 5 = 5 x 9   (f) 6 x 7 = 7 x 6

4. Fill in the missing numbers.

   (a) 9 x 6 = _____ x _____ = _____   (b) 10 x 5 = _____ x _____ = _____
   (c) 10 x 4 = _____ x _____ = _____   (d) 4 x 8 = _____ x _____ = _____
   (e) 8 x 2 = _____ x _____ = _____   (f) 6 x 7 = _____ x _____ = _____
   (g) 6 x 5 = _____ x _____ = _____   (h) 3 x 9 = _____ x _____ = _____

5.

| 6 x 3 | 5 x 8 | 20 | 10 x 2 | 3 x 6 | 2 x 10 | 63 |

| 4 x 5 | 8 x 5 | 20 | 5 x 4 |
| 18 | 7 x 9 | 9 x 7 | 40 |

6 x 3	=	3 x	=	
	=		=	
	=		=	
	=		=	
	=		=	

Fill the boxes using the above cards. The first one is started for you.

Multiplication

1.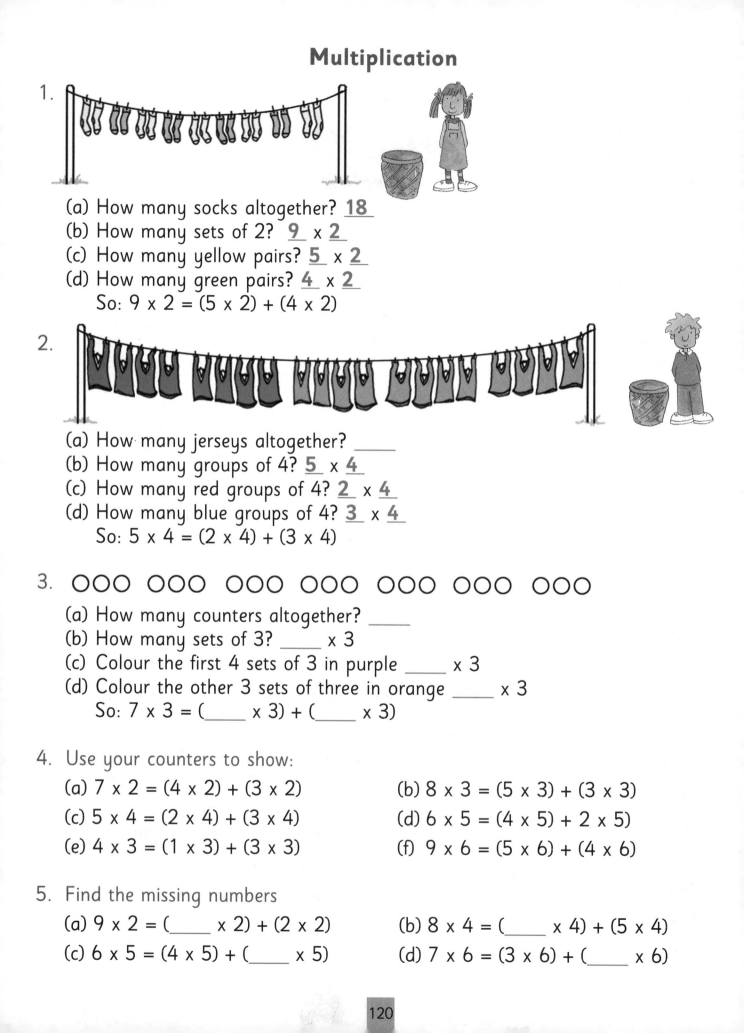

   (a) How many socks altogether? __18__
   (b) How many sets of 2? __9__ x __2__
   (c) How many yellow pairs? __5__ x __2__
   (d) How many green pairs? __4__ x __2__
       So: 9 x 2 = (5 x 2) + (4 x 2)

2.

   (a) How many jerseys altogether? _____
   (b) How many groups of 4? __5__ x __4__
   (c) How many red groups of 4? __2__ x __4__
   (d) How many blue groups of 4? __3__ x __4__
       So: 5 x 4 = (2 x 4) + (3 x 4)

3. ○○○ ○○○ ○○○ ○○○ ○○○ ○○○ ○○○

   (a) How many counters altogether? _____
   (b) How many sets of 3? _____ x 3
   (c) Colour the first 4 sets of 3 in purple _____ x 3
   (d) Colour the other 3 sets of three in orange _____ x 3
       So: 7 x 3 = (_____ x 3) + (_____ x 3)

4. Use your counters to show:
   (a) 7 x 2 = (4 x 2) + (3 x 2)   (b) 8 x 3 = (5 x 3) + (3 x 3)
   (c) 5 x 4 = (2 x 4) + (3 x 4)   (d) 6 x 5 = (4 x 5) + 2 x 5)
   (e) 4 x 3 = (1 x 3) + (3 x 3)   (f) 9 x 6 = (5 x 6) + (4 x 6)

5. Find the missing numbers
   (a) 9 x 2 = (_____ x 2) + (2 x 2)   (b) 8 x 4 = (_____ x 4) + (5 x 4)
   (c) 6 x 5 = (4 x 5) + (_____ x 5)   (d) 7 x 6 = (3 x 6) + (_____ x 6)

120

Match the circles

10 x 7   7 x 7   3 x 7

These three yellow circles match because
10 x 7 = (7 x 7) + (3 x 7)

Look at each of the coloured circles below and find the other two circles to match them. Colour the matching circles.

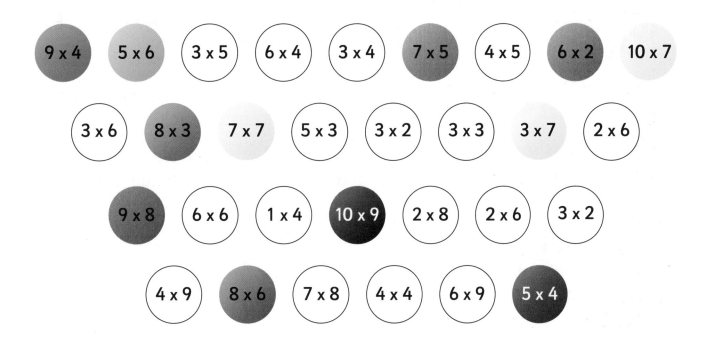

Now write the numbers from the matching circles below.

Yellow: **10 x 7 = (7 x 7) + (3 x 7) = 70**

Orange: 5 x 6 = (__ x __) + (__ x __) = ___

Blue: _____

Green: _____

Red: _____

Pink: _____

Brown: _____

Black: _____

Purple: _____

Navy: _____

You need:
- interlocking cubes
- to practise all division facts

Bigger numbers

1. Divide these 48 cubes equally between Jason and Matthew.

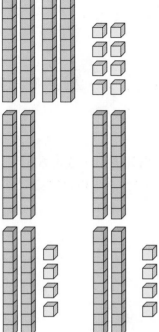

48 = 4 tens and 8 units.

First divide the tens between them. Each boy gets 2 tens or 20 units each.

Now divide the 8 units between them. Each of them gets 4 units.

Altogether they get 2 tens and 4 units each. They get 24 cubes each. You can write it as a division sentence in 2 ways like this:

$$48 \div 2 = 24 \quad \textbf{or} \quad 2 \overline{\smash{\big)}48} \atop \;24$$

2. Share 45 cubes among three children.

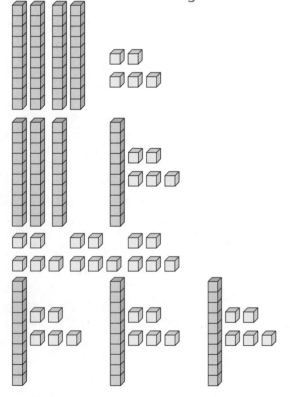

45 = 4 tens and 5 units

First divide the tens among them. Each child gets 1 ten. And there is one ten left over.

Change that ten into units. Now there are 15 units to be shared. Each of them gets 5 units.

Altogether they get 1 ten and 5 units each. You can write it as a division sentence in 2 ways like this:

$$45 \div 3 = 15 \quad \textbf{or} \quad 3 \overline{\smash{\big)}4^{1}5} \atop \;15$$

Sharing with larger numbers

1. Share 54 cubes among three children. Draw the cubes yourself.

First divide the tens among them.
Each child gets 1 ten.
And there are two tens left over.

Change the two tens into units.
Now there are 24 units to be shared.
Each of them gets 8 units.

Altogether they get 18 cubes each.
Now write it as a division sentence
in 2 ways:

_____ ÷ _____ = 18 **or**   ⌐__

2. Use your cubes to help you with the following questions.
   Write a division sentence for each story using the two ways.

(a) Daddy gave 50c to Joan to share with Michael.
    How much did each of them get?

$50 \div 2 =$ ___c **or** 2⌐50
                            ___c

(b) Divide 36 bananas equally between 2 monkeys.

___ ÷ ___ = ___ **or**   ⌐__

(c) The teacher had 54 sweets. She gave 3 sweets to
    each child in the class. How many children were there?

___ ÷ ___ = ___ **or**   ⌐__

(d) 3 children shared 75c among them. How much did each child get?

___ ÷ ___ = ___ **or**   ⌐__

Sharing with remainders

1. You may use your cubes to do these questions.

   (a) 30 ÷ 2 = ___   (b) 54 ÷ 2 = ___   (c) 48 ÷ 3 = ___   (d) 72 ÷ 3 = ___

   (e) 52 ÷ 4 = ___   (f) 60 ÷ 4 = ___   (g) 75 ÷ 5 = ___   (h) 90 ÷ 5 = ___

   (i) 72 ÷ 6 = ___   (j) 84 ÷ 6 = ___   (k) 84 ÷ 7 = ___   (l) 96 ÷ 8 = ___

2. Do these the short way. The first one is done for you.

   (a) 2 | 52   (b) 3 | 75   (c) 4 | 56   (d) 4 | 96
       26

   (e) 5 | 85   (f) 5 | 65   (g) 6 | 78   (h) 6 | 90

   (i) 7 | 91   (j) 7 | 98   (k) 8 | 96   (l) 7 | 84

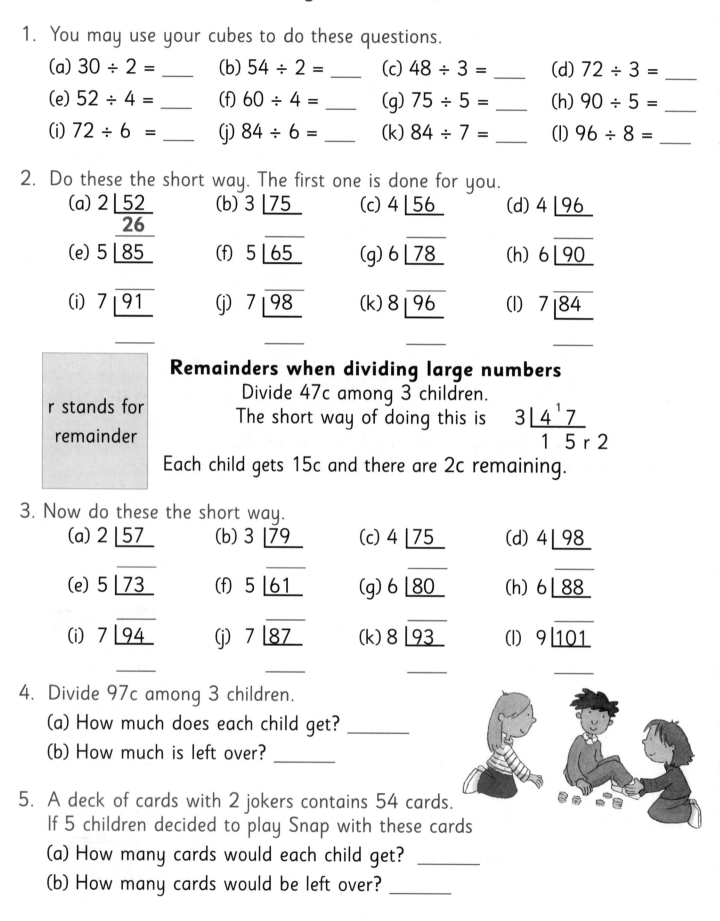

r stands for remainder

Remainders when dividing large numbers
Divide 47c among 3 children.
The short way of doing this is $3 \underline{| 4\,^1 7}$
                                       $1\ \ 5\ r\ 2$
Each child gets 15c and there are 2c remaining.

3. Now do these the short way.

   (a) 2 | 57   (b) 3 | 79   (c) 4 | 75   (d) 4 | 98

   (e) 5 | 73   (f) 5 | 61   (g) 6 | 80   (h) 6 | 88

   (i) 7 | 94   (j) 7 | 87   (k) 8 | 93   (l) 9 | 101

4. Divide 97c among 3 children.

   (a) How much does each child get? _____

   (b) How much is left over? _____

5. A deck of cards with 2 jokers contains 54 cards.
   If 5 children decided to play Snap with these cards

   (a) How many cards would each child get? _____

   (b) How many cards would be left over? _____

Problems for you to solve

1. There are 95 children in Bridgetown School. How many 7-a-side teams can be made and how many children will be left without being on a team? _____ , _____

2.  The teacher bought a big box of 100 crayons. She gave 8 crayons to each group. How many groups were there and how many crayons were left over? _____ , _____

3. I have 75 sweets. How many children will get 4 sweets each and how many sweets will be left over? _____ , _____

Who fell off the wall?

The answers to all these questions are written on the bricks of the wall. With your pencil shade the bricks with the correct answers and you will find the initials of a famous character who fell off a wall once upon a time.

(a) 2 |54 ___

(b) 3 |72 ___

(c) 4 |68 ___

(d) 4 |92 ___

(e) 5 |95 ___

(f) 5 |80 ___

(g) 6 |84 ___

(h) 6 |72 ___

(i) 7 |93 ___

(j) 8 |122 ___

(k) 8 |99 ___

(l) 9 |104 ___

(m) 5|96 ___

(n) 6 |99 ___

(o) 7 |92 ___

25	18	20	11	31	18r4	19r4	35	32r1	30
13	29	13r1	26	16	22r2	16r3	14	11r5	1r3
12r5	13r4	12	19r1	24	33	17	21r2	27	17r4
27r4	16r1	15r2	10r4	19	15r5	23	13r2	12r3	14r5

125

Estimation

1.  Guess the number of paintbrushes in the jar.

   Sensible guess **10**   Wild guess **769**   Answer **12**

2. Guess how many cards are held in the hand.

   Sensible guess _____   Wild guess _____   Answer _____

3. Guess how many apples are in the box.

   Sensible guess _____   Wild guess _____   Answer _____

A sensible guess is called an estimate

4. Put the following things on your table. Estimate how many are in each and then count to find the exact number in each.

   (a) a handful of counters   (b) a container of crayons   (c) a pile of copybooks

   Estimate _____   Estimate _____   Estimate _____

   Answer _____   Answer _____   Answer _____

5. Rounding up or down to the nearest ten or hundred helps to estimate answers.

   (a) 156 + 32   Estimate **160** + **30** = **190**   Answer **188**

   (b) 416 + 276   Estimate _____ + _____ = _____   Answer _____

   (c) 48 – 21   Estimate **50** – **20** = _____   Answer _____

   (d) 196 – 84   Estimate _____ – _____ = _____   Answer _____

   (e) 17 x 3   Estimate **20** x **3** = _____   Answer _____

   (f) 37 x 6   Estimate _____ x **6** = _____   Answer _____

   (g) 87 ÷ 9   Estimate **90** ÷ **10** = _____   Answer _____

   (h) 73 ÷ 10   Estimate _____ ÷ _____ = _____   Answer _____

6. Estimate these and compare your estimate with the correct answer.

   (a) The number of windows in your school.   Estimate _____   Answer _____

   (b) The number of doors in your school.   Estimate _____   Answer _____

   (c) The number of children in your school. Estimate _____   Answer _____

Fun with numbers

Across

1. 25 + 15 = _____
2. 12 x 3 = _____
3. 124 ÷ 4 = _____
4. 316 – 48 = _____
5. 400 – 150 = _____
7. 192 ÷ 8 = _____
9. 39 x 2 = _____
10. 8 x 4 = _____
11. 100 – 25 = _____
12. 132 ÷ 6 = _____
13. 18 + 12 + 8 = _____
14. 200 ÷ 4 = _____

Down

1. 8 x 6 = _____
2. 400 – 52 = _____
3. 124 + 221 = _____
5. 24 x 10 = _____
6. 184 ÷ 2 = _____
8. 46 x 2 = _____
9. 312 ÷ 4 = _____
10. 100 + 200 + 48 = _____
11. 999 – 278 = _____
13. 141 – 102 = _____

You need:
- 1kg bag of sugar   - a balance
- different weights: 500g, 200g, 100g, 50g, 10g and 5g
- the items required for Q2 on this page

1. Take a bag of sugar in your hand.
    Feel the weight of it. It weighs 1kg.
    There are 1000 grammes in 1kg.
    Now take a full schoolbag in your other hand.
    Feel the weight of the bag.
    Would you say that the schoolbag is **lighter**,
    heavier or the **same weight** as the bag
    of sugar? _____

2. Now your teacher will select 8 items from the classroom or school
    and you have to estimate whether they are **heavier**, **lighter** or
    the **same weight** as the 1kg bag of sugar. Then you can use the
    balance to check the answers. The items are

- milk (1 litre)
- this mathematics book
- 3 apples or 3 oranges
- a mug

- full lunchbox
- flower vase
- jar of colouring paint
- a glass of water

This symbol < means **smaller than**
This symbol > means **greater than**

Put a tick (✓) to show your answers.

Item		My estimate			When I put on balance		
		< 1kg	> 1kg	= 1kg	< 1kg	> 1kg	= 1kg
1.	milk						
2.	maths book						
3.	apples/oranges						
4.	a mug						
5.	lunch box						
6.	flower vase						
7.	jar of paint						
8.	a glass of water						

Kilogrammes and grammes

1. When you are at home, find the 6 items that are listed below. Estimate their weights when they have not been opened and write them in the table below. Then find the actual weights that are written on the items.

	Item	Estimate	Actual weight
1.	Salt		
2.	Tea		
3.	Flour		
4.	Butter		
5.	Jam		
6.	Biscuits		

2. Now see if you can do the same with 5 items that are in the school or classroom. Record your results in a table in your copy.

3. We use **kilogrammes (kg)** to measure the weight of **heavy** things and **grammes (g)** to measure the weight of **light** things. Which unit of measurement would you use for the following items?

	Item	Unit (kg or g)
1.	Bag of potatoes	
2.	An apple	
3.	Cheese	
4.	A bag of coal	
5.	Cornflakes	
6.	History book	
7.	Loaf of bread	
8.	Chicken	

4. Put these creatures in order beginning with the lightest.
   hippopotamus, pig, cat, horse, rabbit, rat, mouse, blue whale, cow, dog

   _____, _____, _____, _____, _____,

   _____, _____, _____, _____, _____,

Heavy and light

1. Which item is the heaviest? _____

2. Which item is the lightest? _____

3. What is the difference in weight between the heaviest and the lightest?

   _____

4. Which is the biggest item? _____

5. Which is the smallest item? _____

6. Is the biggest item the heaviest? _____

7. Is the smallest item the lightest? _____

8. If you put the cornflakes on the balance, what weights would you need
   to level the balance? _____ Do the same with the biscuits. _____

9. What weights would you need to balance the butter and the cornflakes?

   _____

10. Which 3 items add up to 1kg altogether? (There are two answers.)
    (a)_____, _____, _____
    (b)_____, _____, _____

11. What is the total weight of the 6 items above? _____

12. Put the 6 items in order beginning with the lightest.

    _____, _____, _____, _____, _____, _____,

Addition of kilogrammes and grammes

(a)
```
  kg    g
   2   270
 + 3   580
 ─────────
   5   850
```
Ans: 5kg 850g

(b)
```
  kg    g
   2   850
 + 3   560
 ─────────
   6   410
```
Ans: 6kg 410g

(c)
```
  kg    g
   3   590
 + 2,  676
 ─────────
   6   266
```
Ans: 6kg 266g

1. Now try these.

(a)
```
  kg    g
   2   560
 + 3   420
 ─────────
```

(b)
```
  kg    g
   3   780
 + 2   160
 ─────────
```

(c)
```
  kg    g
   4   290
 + 3   660
 ─────────
```

(d)
```
  kg    g
   5   280
 + 3   490
 ─────────
```

(e)
```
  kg    g
   2   650
 + 3   850
 ─────────
```

(f)
```
  kg    g
   5   390
 + 2   790
 ─────────
```

(g)
```
  kg    g
   4   840
 + 3   375
 ─────────
```

(h)
```
  kg    g
   6   290
 + 3   864
 ─────────
```

2. Now try these.

(a)
```
  kg    g
   3   496
   2    84
 + 1   187
 ─────────
```

(b)
```
  kg    g
   3   780
   1   195
 + 2    84
 ─────────
```

(c)
```
  kg    g
   6    39
   4   196
 + 5   395
 ─────────
```

(d)
```
  kg    g
   4    93
   3   186
 + 2   295
 ─────────
```

3. Do these in your copybook.

(a) 2kg 360g + 4kg 98g

(b) 6kg 84g + 3kg 985g

(c) 2kg 840g + 5kg 28g

(d) 8kg 98g + 3kg 970g

(e) 4kg 28g + 3kg 960g + 2kg 96g

(f) 4kg 36g + 2kg 840g + 2kg 98g

Subtraction of kilogrammes and grammes

(a)
```
  kg      g
   2     968
 - 1     246
 ─────────────
   1     722
```
Ans: 1kg 722g

(b)
```
  kg      g
  ³ 11 13 ¹
   4     242
 - 1     396
 ─────────────
   2     846
```
Ans: 2kg 846g

(c)
```
  kg      g
  ² 11 17 ¹
   3     280
 - 1     496
 ─────────────
   1     784
```
Ans: 1kg 784g

1. Now try these.

(a)
```
  kg      g
   4     876
 - 2     345
 ─────────────
```

(b)
```
  kg      g
   5     798
 - 3     286
 ─────────────
```

(c)
```
  kg      g
   6     242
 - 4     521
 ─────────────
```

(d)
```
  kg      g
   9     365
 - 6     482
 ─────────────
```

(e)
```
  kg      g
   4     262
 - 2     584
 ─────────────
```

(f)
```
  kg      g
   5     550
 - 2     986
 ─────────────
```

(g)
```
  kg      g
   6     500
 - 2     976
 ─────────────
```

(h)
```
  kg      g
   8     250
 - 2     786
 ─────────────
```

From 3kg take 1kg 867g

```
  kg      g
  ² ⁹ ⁹ ¹
   3     000
 - 1     867
 ─────────────
   1     133
```
Ans: 1kg 133g

2. Now try these.

(a)
```
  kg      g
   3     000
 - 1     759
 ─────────────
```

(b)
```
  kg      g
   4     000
 - 2     366
 ─────────────
```

(c)
```
  kg      g
   5     000
 - 2     840
 ─────────────
```

(d)
```
  kg      g
   7     000
 - 2      85
 ─────────────
```

3. Do these in your copybook.

   (a) 3kg – 1kg 96g   (b) 4kg – 2kg 306g   (c) 6kg – 4kg 370g
   (d) 7kg – 2kg 500g   (e) $7\frac{1}{2}$kg – 3kg 295g   (f) $8\frac{1}{4}$kg – 200kg

Problems for you to solve

1. John's father posted 2 parcels yesterday. The first parcel weighed 3kg 750g and the second weighed 4kg 360g. What is the total weight of the 2 parcels? _____

2. Michelle's aunt baked a cake last Christmas. She put in 750g of currants, 800g of sultanas and 250g of raisins. How much fruit altogether did she put in the cake? _____

3. The McEvoys had a luggage allowance of 16kg when they were flying to Spain on their holidays. When their cases were weighed at the airport they were 21kg 200g. How much overweight were the cases? _____

4. Deirdre's dog weighs 8kg 250g. Paula's dog weighs only 6kg 500g. What is the difference in the weight of the 2 dogs? _____

5. One bag weighs 5kg and another bag weighs 3kg 650g. What is the difference in the weight of the 2 bags? _____

Do you know?

Which is heavier: 10kg of coal or 10kg of feathers? _____

133

You need:
- 3-D shapes   - colouring pencils
- nets for 3-D shapes
- to explain vertices

(a) sphere   (b) cone   (c) triangular prism

(d) cube   (e) cuboid   (f) cylinder   (g) pyramid

1. Colour the shapes and describe them below. The first one is done for you.

(a) __a red sphere_____   (b) _____

(c) _____   (d) _____

(e) _____   (f) _____

(g) _____

At the circus

2. Look closely at the picture.

(a) Colour the triangular prism green.

(b) All cones are to be coloured red.

(c) Find the two cylinders and colour them yellow.

(d) The pyramid is to be purple.

(e) Can you see a cube? Colour it blue.

(f) Make sure all spheres are different colours.

(g) Cuboids are to be coloured yellow.

(h) Now colour in the rest of the picture.

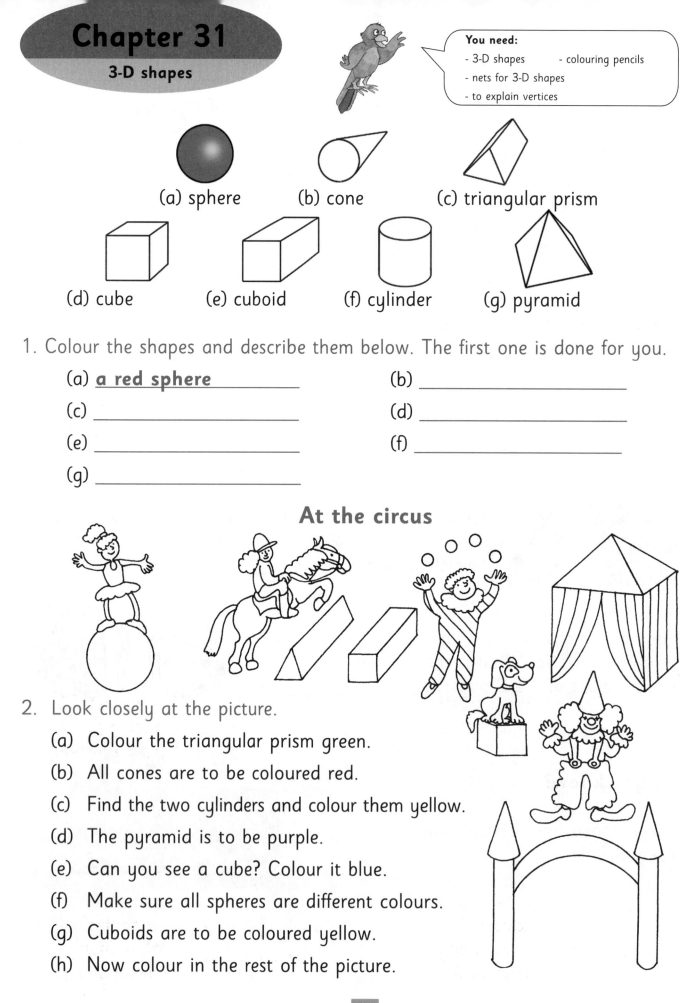

Faces and vertices

1. Look at this dice. What shape is it? _____
    There is one dot on the pink face.
    Put 5 dots on this face and colour it blue.
    Put 3 dots on this face and colour it green.
    How many faces can you see? _____
    How many corners or vertices can you see? ___

2. You need a dice or another cube to answer these questions.
    (a) How many faces has a cube? _____
    (b) How many corners or vertices has a cube? _____
    (c) Are the faces of the cube flat or curved? _____

3. Put a cube ⬜, a cuboid ▱, a triangular prism ◺, and a pyramid △
    on your table. Use them to fill this grid.

	Number of faces	Number of vertices
Cube		
Cuboid		
Triangular prism		
Pyramid		

4. These nets can be folded to make shapes. Look at each net and write the
    shape you think it makes into the box. Then answer the questions.

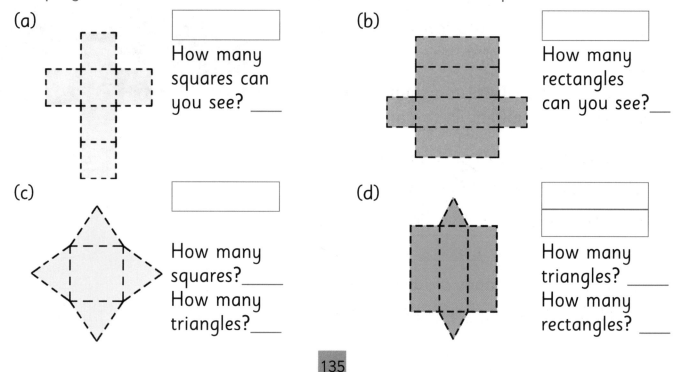

(a) [____]
How many
squares can
you see? ___

(b) [____]
How many
rectangles
can you see?__

(c) [____]
How many
squares?____
How many
triangles?___

(d) [____]
How many
triangles? ____
How many
rectangles? ___

Flat or curved

1. You now need a cylinder, a cone and a pyramid on your table. You will notice flat faces and curved faces. Use the shapes to help you fill in the missing numbers below.

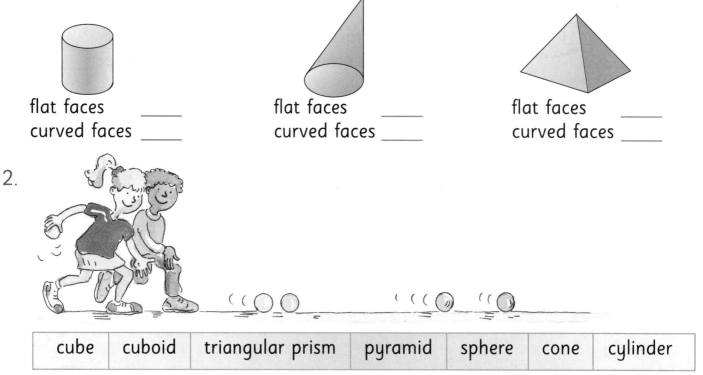

flat faces ____   flat faces ____   flat faces ____
curved faces ____   curved faces ____   curved faces ____

2.

| cube | cuboid | triangular prism | pyramid | sphere | cone | cylinder |

(a) Work with a partner now and see how many of these shapes will roll. Put ✔ in the grid below if the shape rolls and ✗ if it does not roll.

(b) Now try stacking a few of each shape and fill in the grid below.

(c) Find out how well the shapes slide and fill in the final line in the grid.

roll							
stack							
slide							

3. Make some 3D shapes of your own using cardboard nets. Fold them to make the shapes.

Fun with 3-D shapes

1.

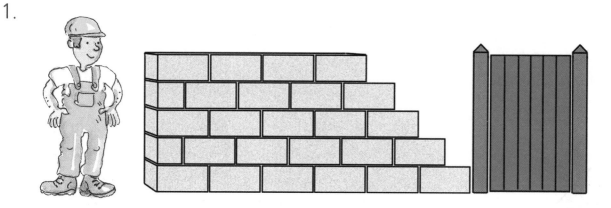

(a) What shape are the bricks? _____

(b) The builder has run out of bricks! How many bricks
   does he need to finish the wall? _____

2. Put four unit cubes on your table like this.
   Use more cubes on top to build a cube.
   How many unit cubes have you used? _____

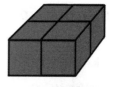

3. This time use 9 unit cubes for the base.
   Keep building until you have made a large cube.
   How many unit cubes did you use? _____

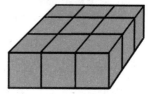

4. Use 8 unit cubes to make this shape on your table.
   Put another 8 cubes on top.
   What shape have you built? _____

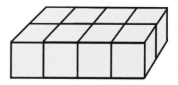

5. Sheila saw a small display of coke
   cans like this in the supermarket.
   She drew a picture of a similar
   display but she put 6 cylinders
   in the bottom line. How many cylinders
   did she draw altogether? _____

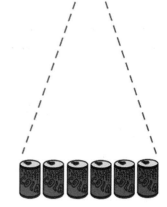

Chapter 32
Lines and angles

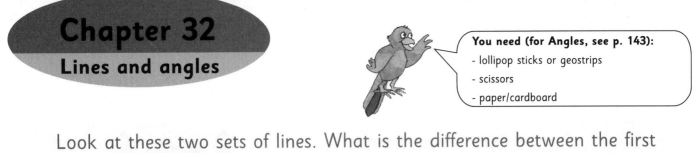

You need (for Angles, see p. 143):
- lollipop sticks or geostrips
- scissors
- paper/cardboard

Look at these two sets of lines. What is the difference between the first set of lines and the second set?

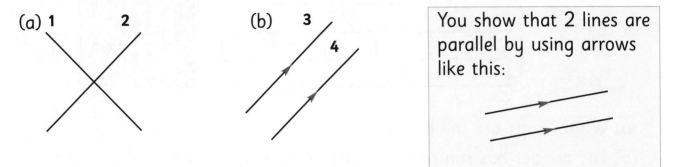

You show that 2 lines are parallel by using arrows like this:

Lines 1 and 2 **intersect**. That means they cross each other. But lines 3 and 4 are **not intersecting**. These lines are **parallel** to each other.

1. Look around the classroom and see if you can find shapes that have parallel lines. Make a list of them here.

   (a) _____   (b) _____

   (c) _____   (d) _____

   (e) _____   (f) _____

2. Draw 2 of these shapes in the boxes below and show the lines that are parallel.

Parallel lines

1. Look at these pictures and pick out the things that are parallel to each other. The first one is done for you.

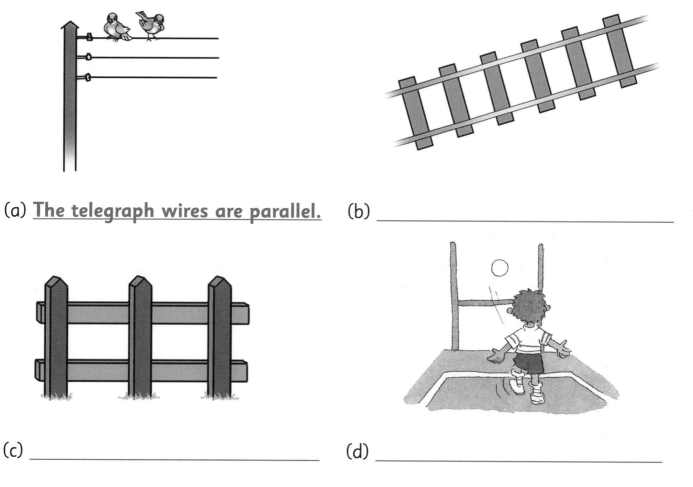

(a) <u>**The telegraph wires are parallel.**</u> (b) _____

(c) _____ (d) _____

2. Use arrows to mark the parallel lines on these shapes.

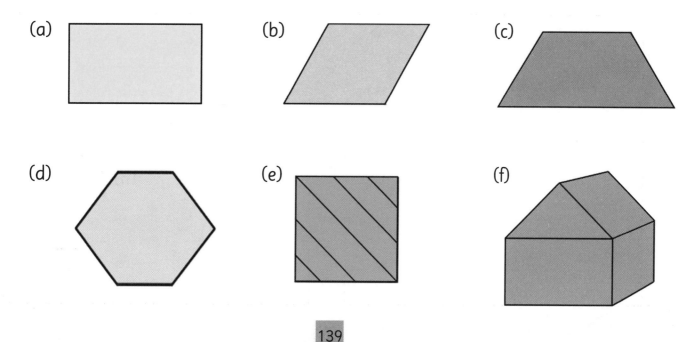

Parallel lines

1. When you draw the 26 capital letters in the alphabet you will discover
   that 6 of them have parallel lines. The first one is the letter E.
   Draw the other 5 in the boxes below.

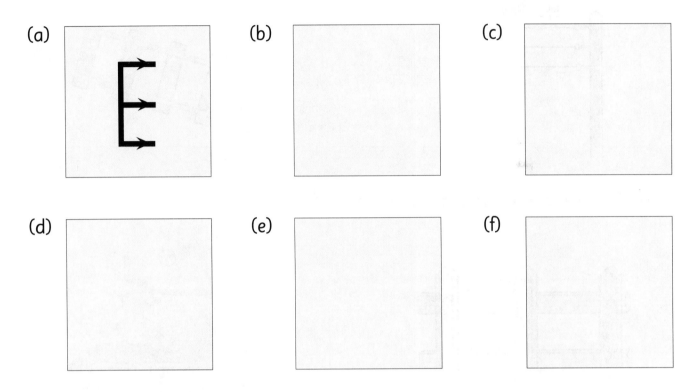

2. There are many numbers less than 50 that have parallel lines.
   The first one is the number four. Write eight more such
   numbers in the boxes below.

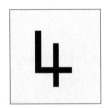

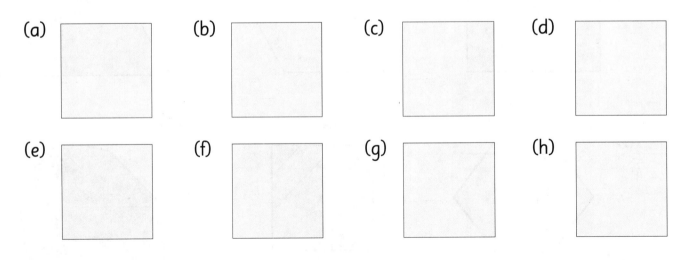

Horizontal and vertical lines

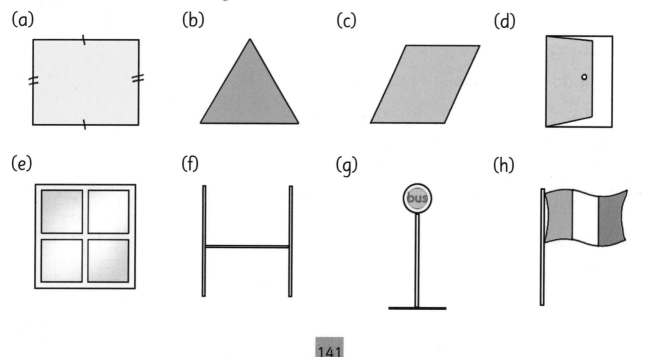

When you are standing up you are in a **vertical** position.

When you are lying down you are in a **horizontal** position.

1. Look at the picture above. Can you pick out and describe

    (a) two horizontal lines? _____

    (b) two vertical lines? _____

2. Now include another two items in the picture: one in a horizontal position and one vertical.

3. Look for horizontal and vertical lines in these shapes. Put one tick (–) on the horizontal lines and two ticks (=) on the vertical lines. The first one is done for you.

(a)   (b)   (c)   (d)

(e)   (f)   (g)   (h)

Horizontal and vertical lines

1. Draw three items in the classroom or at home that have horizontal and vertical lines.

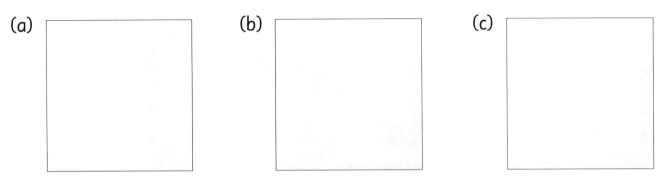

(a)   (b)   (c)

2. Some of the capital letters in the alphabet have horizontal lines and some have vertical lines. But only 5 of them have both. Draw these 5 letters in the boxes below. Put one tick (−) on the horizontal lines and 2 ticks (=) on the vertical lines.

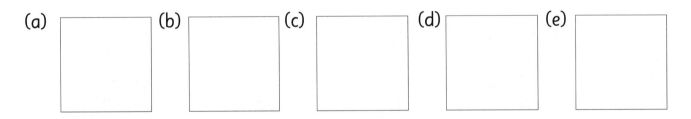

(a)   (b)   (c)   (d)   (e)

True or False?

Tick the correct box (✓)

	T	F
(a) Railway tracks are parallel.	☐	☐
(b) Flag poles are usually horizontal.	☐	☐
(c) The Leaning Tower of Pisa is vertical.	☐	☐
(d) Electricity cables are both horizontal and parallel.	☐	☐
(e) The door is vertical.	☐	☐
(f) The floor is vertical.	☐	☐
(g) Most walls are horizontal.	☐	☐
(h) A rectangle has parallel, horizontal and vertical lines.	☐	☐

Angles

Get 2 lollipop sticks or geostrips. Put them flat on top of each other. Now slide one up a little (as shown in diagram (b)). The space between the two lollipop sticks/geostrips is called an angle. Keep on making the angle bigger and stop when you think you have a corner.

Mark the right angles that you can see.

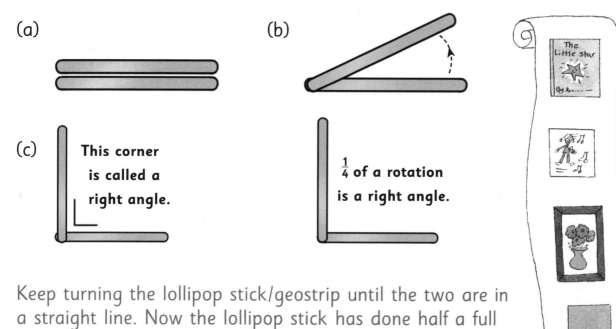

(a)

(b)

(c) **This corner is called a right angle.**

$\frac{1}{4}$ **of a rotation is a right angle.**

Keep turning the lollipop stick/geostrip until the two are in a straight line. Now the lollipop stick has done half a full turn (rotation).

(d)

Keep turning the lollipop stick/geostrip until the two are back in the position they were at the beginning. This is a full turn or rotation.

(e)

Right angles

1. The teacher will ask you to stand up and face the front of the classroom.

   Now turn to the left (anti-clockwise) until your right shoulder is pointing to the front of the classroom. This is a quarter of a rotation, a right angle.

   Now keep turning until your back is to the front of the classroom. This is half a rotation.

   Keep turning until you are back at the position you started. This is a full rotation.

2. Make a right angle. Take a piece of paper and fold it in half and then fold it in half again. Now you have a strong right angle.

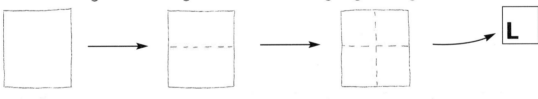

   Use this paper right angle to find right angles in your classroom. See how many you can find in

   (a) your maths book cover   (b) your desk
   (c) the classroom window   (d) the classroom door
   (e) the wall   (f) the blackboard/whiteboard

3. Look at these shapes and mark the places where you find a right angle.

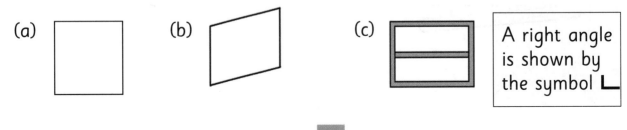

(a)   (b)   (c)   A right angle is shown by the symbol ⌐

Bigger or smaller than right angles

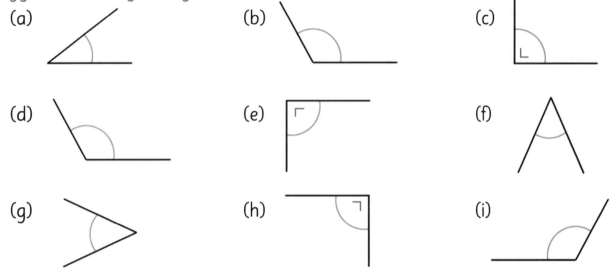

The angle marked 1 is smaller than a right angle. The angle marked 2 is a right angle. The angle that has the number 3 on it is bigger than a right angle.

1. Look at these angles and write 1 on angles that are smaller than a right angle, write 2 on the right angles, and write 3 on the angles that are bigger than a right angle.

    (a)   (b)   (c)

    (d)   (e)   (f)

    (g)   (h)   (i)

2. How many angles can you see in each of these shapes? Write the number of angles in the box beside the shape.

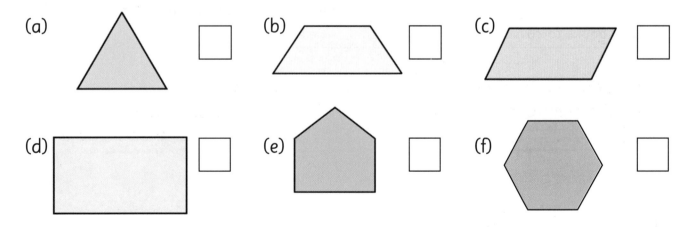

    (a)   (b)   (c)

    (d)   (e)   (f)

    Now write 1 on the angles smaller than a right angle, write 2 on the right angles, and write 3 on the angles bigger than a right angle.

You need:
- colouring pencils   - rulers
- to explain 'surface'
- to explain 'area'
- square is written as sq.

1. The **surface** of the table top, the side of the truck and the wall are being spray painted. The word **area** is used to describe the size of a surface. Of the 3 surfaces, which has the biggest area? _____
Now finish colouring in the three pictures.

2. You are going to cover your table top with copybooks.
Estimate how many copybooks you will use and write your findings below.

	Estimate	Number of copybooks used
copybooks to cover table top		

3. If, instead of copybooks, you used postage stamps to cover the area of your table top, would you need **more** or **less** stamps than copybooks? _____

4. Now cover the table top with maths books. Estimate the number of maths books you will need and record your answers below.

	Estimate	Number of maths books used
maths books to cover table top		

5.

How many square tiles were used to cover this part of the bathroom wall?
___ square tiles

6.

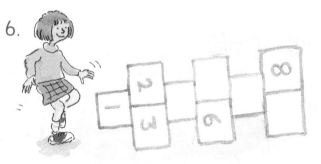

Fill in the missing numbers on this game of hopscotch. How many squares are there in all?
___ squares

We measure area in square units

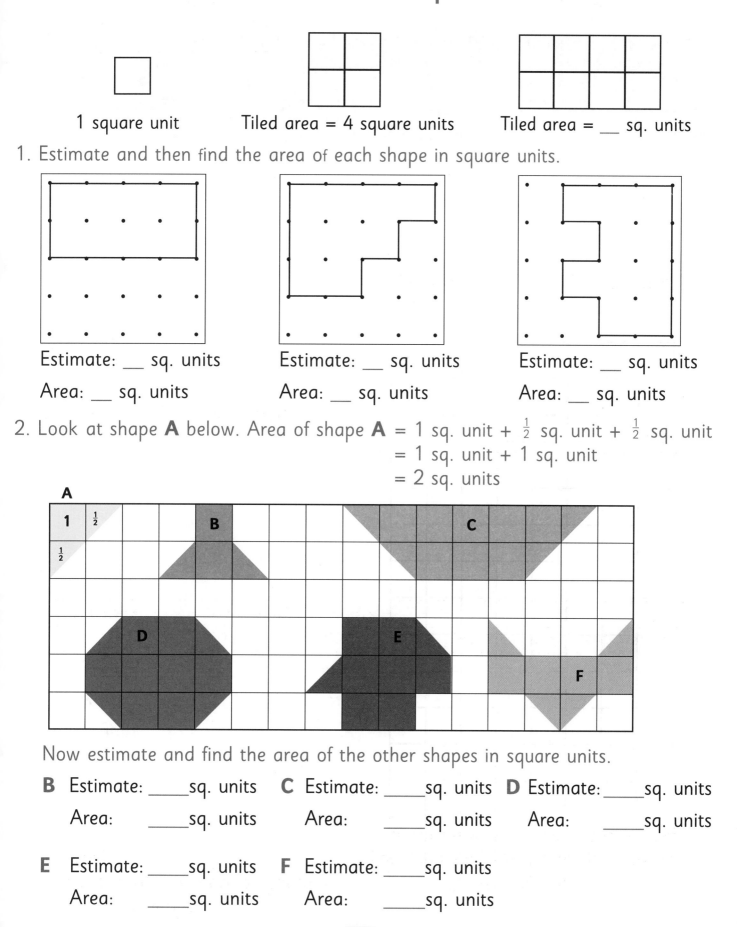

1 square unit   Tiled area = 4 square units   Tiled area = __ sq. units

1. Estimate and then find the area of each shape in square units.

Estimate: __ sq. units   Estimate: __ sq. units   Estimate: __ sq. units

Area: __ sq. units   Area: __ sq. units   Area: __ sq. units

2. Look at shape **A** below. Area of shape **A** = 1 sq. unit + $\frac{1}{2}$ sq. unit + $\frac{1}{2}$ sq. unit
= 1 sq. unit + 1 sq. unit
= 2 sq. units

Now estimate and find the area of the other shapes in square units.

B Estimate: ____ sq. units   **C** Estimate: ____ sq. units   **D** Estimate: ____ sq. units

Area: ____ sq. units   Area: ____ sq. units   Area: ____ sq. units

E Estimate: ____ sq. units   **F** Estimate: ____ sq. units

Area: ____ sq. units   Area: ____ sq. units

Area

1. Draw three shapes to match the areas given below.
   Use a ruler! Then colour the shapes you drew.

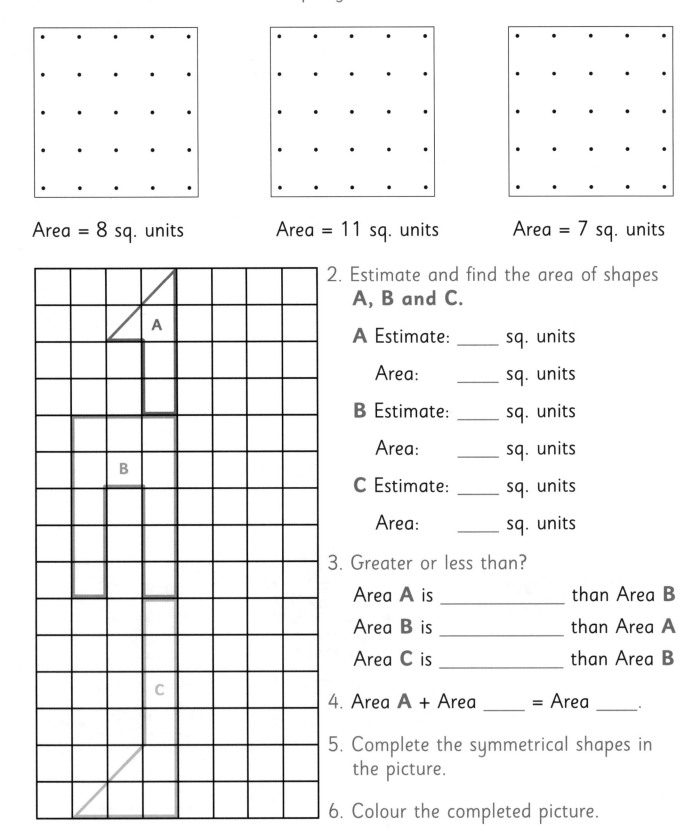

Area = 8 sq. units   Area = 11 sq. units   Area = 7 sq. units

2. Estimate and find the area of shapes **A, B and C.**

   A Estimate: _____ sq. units

   Area: _____ sq. units

   B Estimate: _____ sq. units

   Area: _____ sq. units

   C Estimate: _____ sq. units

   Area: _____ sq. units

3. Greater or less than?

   Area **A** is _____ than Area **B**

   Area **B** is _____ than Area **A**

   Area **C** is _____ than Area **B**

4. Area **A** + Area ____ = Area ____.

5. Complete the symmetrical shapes in the picture.

6. Colour the completed picture.

1. If it is now 9.50, how many minutes to go before 10 o'clock? _____ minutes

2. If it is now a quarter to 4, how many minutes is it after 3 o'clock? _____ minutes

3. 8 x 4 = 4 x _____ = _____   4. 9 x 2 = (6 x _____) + (_____ x 2)

5. If 27 chocolate buttons were shared equally among 5 children, how many buttons would each child get and how many would be left over?
   _____ each   _____ left over

6. 6kg 84g + 3kg 987g = _____   7. 8kg 60g – 2kg 716g = _____

8. How many faces has a cube? _____ faces

9. How many vertices has a cuboid? _____ vertices

10. Name a shape that has a curved face. _____

11. Draw 2 lines that intersect.

12. Draw 2 parallel lines.

13. Draw goalposts and colour the vertical lines blue and the horizontal line red.

14. Colour the right angles in this shape.

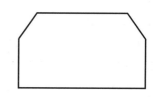

15.

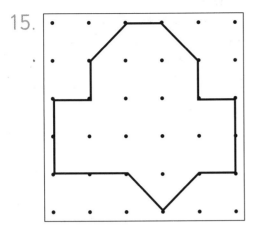

Area of this shape = _____ sq. units

16.

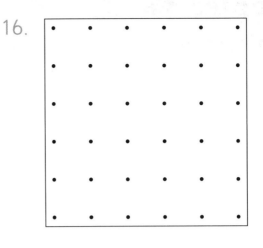

Draw a shape that has an area of 9 sq. units.

17.  The bus left town at 10.05 and arrived at the terminus at 11.15. **How long did the journey take?** _____

18. The man getting on the bus is carrying three packages weighing 2kg 250g, 3kg 560g and 1kg 450g in his bag. **How much weight is he carrying altogether?** _____

19. Anne, Kate and Liam got on the bus and Kate paid the fares. The fare was 60c each. **How much did Kate pay in all?** _____

20. The bus arrived at the shopping centre with 44 passengers on board. One quarter of the passengers got off the bus at this stop. **How many people got off the bus?** _____

How well did you do?

Give yourself 1 mark for each question you answered correctly and then tick the box with your score.

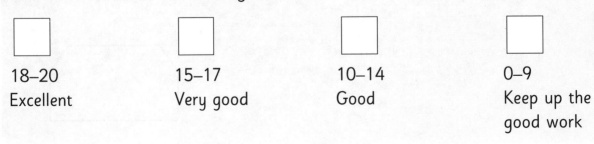

| 18–20 Excellent | 15–17 Very good | 10–14 Good | 0–9 Keep up the good work |

Chapter 35
Capacity

You need:
- 1l, 500ml and 250ml measures.
- various cartons and bottles of different sizes for Q4 and Q5
- a spoon and a cup

1. The **capacity** of a container is the amount of liquid it can hold.
   For example, the **capacity** of this milk carton is 1 litre.
   Can you name other things that come in 1 litre cartons or bottles?
   Make a list of them.

   _____

   _____

2. Now make a list of 8 things that come in cartons or bottles that are
   (a) smaller than 1 litre
   (b) bigger than 1 litre
   The first one in each list is done for you.

	Smaller than 1 litre		Bigger than 1 litre
1	yogurt	1	car oil
2		2	
3		3	
4		4	
5		5	
6		6	
7		7	
8		8	

3. Make a list of 8 liquids that are bought and sold in very large containers. Here is one to help you.

   _petrol,_____

   _____

Millilitres

To measure the capacity of small containers we use millilitres (ml).

There are 1000 millilitres (ml) in 1 litre (l).

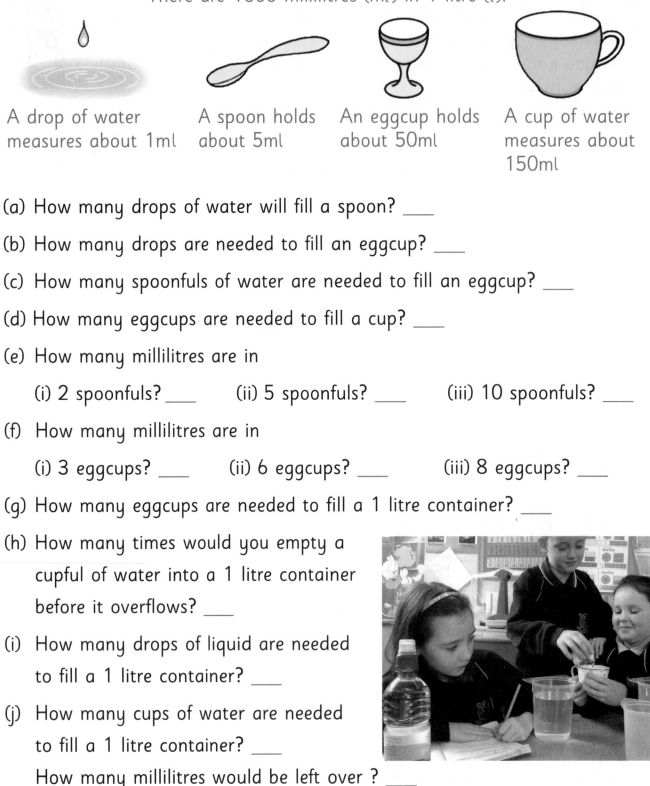

A drop of water measures about 1ml   A spoon holds about 5ml   An eggcup holds about 50ml   A cup of water measures about 150ml

(a) How many drops of water will fill a spoon? ____

(b) How many drops are needed to fill an eggcup? ____

(c) How many spoonfuls of water are needed to fill an eggcup? ____

(d) How many eggcups are needed to fill a cup? ____

(e) How many millilitres are in

    (i) 2 spoonfuls? ____   (ii) 5 spoonfuls? ____   (iii) 10 spoonfuls? ____

(f) How many millilitres are in

    (i) 3 eggcups? ____   (ii) 6 eggcups? ____   (iii) 8 eggcups? ____

(g) How many eggcups are needed to fill a 1 litre container? ____

(h) How many times would you empty a cupful of water into a 1 litre container before it overflows? ____

(i) How many drops of liquid are needed to fill a 1 litre container? ____

(j) How many cups of water are needed to fill a 1 litre container? ____
How many millilitres would be left over ? ____

Estimation

1. Your teacher will put the following 8 containers on display and she will ask you to estimate the capacity of each container. Then she will tell you the actual capacity of each container. Fill in the answers in the table below.

	Container	My estimate	Actual capacity	Difference
1	shampoo bottle			
2	washing up liquid			
3	sauce bottle			
4	orange carton			
5	yogurt carton			
6	window cleaner			
7	bottle of water			
8	cough bottle			

2. Estimate how many litres are needed to fill the following containers.

	Container	My estimate	Actual capacity	Difference
1	bucket			
2	kettle			
3	basin			
4	sink			
5	watering can			

3. Circle the odd one out and say why.

(a) wood, plastic, water, stone _____

(b) bread, butter, jam, milk _____

(c) sugar, salt, vinegar, chips _____

(d) shampoo, toothpaste, soap, towel _____

(e) tyre, petrol, paint, oil _____

Addition

(a) 2l 290ml + 3l 560ml

l	ml
2	290
+ 3	5,60
5	850

Ans: 5l 850ml

(b) 2l 850ml + 4l 690ml

l	ml
2	850
+ 4,	6,90
7	540

Ans: 7l 540ml

(c) 3l 480ml + 4l 679ml

l	ml
3	480
+ 4,	6,79
8	159

Ans: 8l 159ml

1. Try these.

(a)
l	ml
2	660
+ 3	220

(b)
l	ml
3	780
+ 2	160

(c)
l	ml
4	290
+ 3	670

(d)
l	ml
5	280
+ 3	590

(e)
l	ml
2	650
+ 3	850

(f)
l	ml
5	390
+ 2	890

(g)
l	ml
4	840
+ 3	375

(h)
l	ml
6	595
+ 2	740

2. Now try these.

(a)
l	ml
3	496
2	94
+ 1	187

(b)
l	ml
2	484
1	195
+ 2	64

(c)
l	ml
6	49
4	196
+ 5	295

(d)
l	ml
4	93
3	287
+ 2	395

3. Do these in your copy.

(a) 2l 360ml + 4l 98ml

(b) 6l 84ml + 3l 985ml

(c) 2l 840ml + 5l 28ml

(d) 8l 98ml + 3l 960ml

(e) 4l 28ml + 3l 960ml + 2l 96ml

(f) 5l 36ml + 2l 840ml + 1l 79ml

(g) 6l 28ml + 2l 848ml + 2l 74ml

(h) 3l 360ml + 2l 89ml + 3l 740ml

(i) 5l 792ml + 3l 96ml + 4l 709ml

(j) 6l 394ml + 2l 9ml + 3l 78ml

Subtraction

(a) 2l 868ml – 1l 246ml   (b) 4l 242ml – 1l 396ml (c) 3l 280ml – 1l 496ml

l	ml
2	868
−1	246
1	622

l	ml
³4	¹¹¹³¹242
−1	396
2	846

l	ml
²3	¹¹¹⁷¹280
−1	496
1	784

Ans: 1l 622ml   **Ans:** 2l 846ml   **Ans:** 1l 784ml

1. Try these.

(a) l	ml	(b) l	ml	(c) l	ml	(d) l	ml
4	876	5	798	6	242	9	365
− 2	345	− 3	286	− 4	521	− 6	482

(e) l	ml	(f) l	ml	(g) l	ml	(h) l	ml
4	262	5	350	6	500	8	50
− 2	584	− 2	986	− 2	976	− 2	786

(a) From 3l take 1l 785ml   (b) From 4l take 2l 396ml

l	ml
²3	⁹⁹¹000
−1	785
1	215

l	ml
³4	⁹⁹¹000
−2	396
1	604

2. Now try these.

(a) l	ml	(b) l	ml	(c) l	ml	(d) l	ml
3	000	4	000	5	000	7	000
− 1	759	−2	366	−2	840	− 2	85

(a) l	ml	(f) l	ml	(g) l	ml	(h) l	ml
3	000	4	000	8	000	5	000
− 1	94	−2	506	−5	34	− 1	7

Problems for you to solve

1. There were 5l 500ml of water in the basin
   but Michael accidentally spilled 1l 750ml of it.
   How much water was left in the basin? _____

2.  Sylvia's Dad had 1½ litres of petrol in the
   lawnmower and he put in 3l 750ml more.
   **How much petrol was in the lawnmower
   then?** _____

3. The O'Briens had 85 litres of oil in the oil
   tank. They ordered a delivery of 250 litres.
   How many litres were in the tank then?
   _____

4.  Valerie bought a bottle containing 500ml of
   orange. She drank 285ml of it. **How much
   orange was left in the bottle?** _____

5. Gemma went on a picnic with her family.
   The flask contained 1l 200ml of tea.
   Gemma's mother poured 300ml of tea into
   her mug. **How much tea was left in the flask?**
   _____

6.  Mammy was preparing the dinner and she
   needed exactly 300ml of water. She only
   had jugs that measured 500ml and 200ml.
   Could you help her?
   Write down how you would solve the
   problem. _____
   _____
   _____

You need:
- colouring pencils
- a watch for timing activities

Wednesday's TV Programmes

6.00   Good News and Great Weather Forecast

6.30   Cartoon Time

7.00   Westenders

7.45   The Brennans

8.30   Cook's Corner

9.00   Better News and Weather

9.25   Film: Barry Cotter's Nightmare!

11.00   Best News Ever

11.20   Enemies

11.40   Closedown

Read the timetable and answer the following questions.

1. The shortest programme lasted _____ minutes.

2. The longest programme lasted _____ hour _____ minutes

3. Gráinne watched Westenders and The Brennans. How long was she watching TV? _____ hour _____ minutes

4. Maeve went out with her friends as The Brennans started.
    She came back just as Better News came on. How long was she out?
    _____ hour _____ minutes

5. Dad fell asleep while watching the film! He woke just as
    Enemies started. How long had the film been over? _____ minutes

6. How many news programmes were there on Wednesday night? _____

7. The news programmes lasted _____ hour _____ minutes altogether.

8. Westenders is shown two nights a week. How long is that in all?
    _____ hour _____ minutes

9. The television was switched off at 11.40. Tom's older brother
    went to bed 20 minutes later. What time did he go to bed? _____ o'clock.

Hours and minutes

A football match started at 3 o'clock and finished at a quarter past four.
How long was that in all?

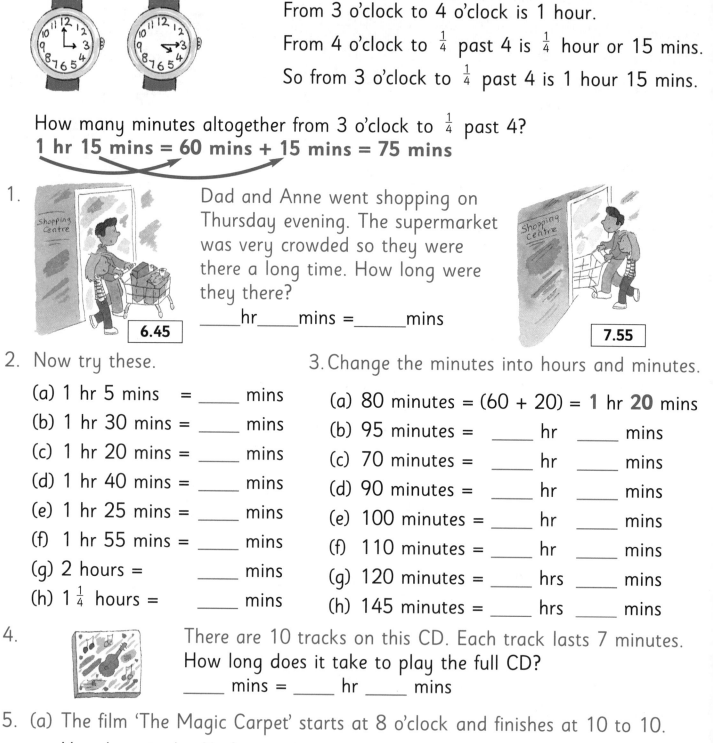

From 3 o'clock to 4 o'clock is 1 hour.

From 4 o'clock to $\frac{1}{4}$ past 4 is $\frac{1}{4}$ hour or 15 mins.

So from 3 o'clock to $\frac{1}{4}$ past 4 is 1 hour 15 mins.

How many minutes altogether from 3 o'clock to $\frac{1}{4}$ past 4?
1 hr 15 mins = 60 mins + 15 mins = 75 mins

1. Dad and Anne went shopping on Thursday evening. The supermarket was very crowded so they were there a long time. How long were they there?

   _____hr_____mins = _____mins

   6.45

   7.55

2. Now try these.

   (a) 1 hr 5 mins   = _____ mins
   (b) 1 hr 30 mins = _____ mins
   (c) 1 hr 20 mins = _____ mins
   (d) 1 hr 40 mins = _____ mins
   (e) 1 hr 25 mins = _____ mins
   (f) 1 hr 55 mins = _____ mins
   (g) 2 hours = _____ mins
   (h) 1 $\frac{1}{4}$ hours = _____ mins

3. Change the minutes into hours and minutes.

   (a) 80 minutes = (60 + 20) = **1** hr **20** mins
   (b) 95 minutes = _____ hr _____ mins
   (c) 70 minutes = _____ hr _____ mins
   (d) 90 minutes = _____ hr _____ mins
   (e) 100 minutes = _____ hr _____ mins
   (f) 110 minutes = _____ hr _____ mins
   (g) 120 minutes = _____ hrs _____ mins
   (h) 145 minutes = _____ hrs _____ mins

4. There are 10 tracks on this CD. Each track lasts 7 minutes. How long does it take to play the full CD?

   _____ mins = _____ hr _____ mins

5. (a) The film 'The Magic Carpet' starts at 8 o'clock and finishes at 10 to 10.

   How long is the film? _____ hr _____ mins = _____ mins

   (b) Anne and her family arrived home 30 minutes after the film ended.

   What time did they get home? _____ : _____

Meet the busy family

			JULY			
M	**T**	**W**	**T**	**F**	**S**	**S**
	1	2	3	4	5	6
7	8	9	10	11	12	13
14	15	16	17	18	19	20
21	22	23	24	25	26	27
28	29	30	31			

Read these questions and fill in the calendar to help the Busy Family to remember all the things they must do in July.

1. (a) 1st July falls on a _____ (b) The last day in June was a _____

2. (a) 24th July is a _____ (b) 1st August is a _____

3. Bob Busy has football training every Saturday. Draw a football on all the Saturdays. **How many training sessions are there in July?** _____

4. Barbara goes to dancing classes every Wednesday. Draw her dancing shoes in all the boxes for Wednesday. **How many dancing classes are there in July?** _____

5. Baby Busy will be one year old on 14th July. Draw a cake on the box for his birthday. **On what day will his birthday fall?** _____

6. Bob and Barbara are going to Summer Camp from Monday to Friday in the third week of July. Write S.C. for summer camp in the correct boxes.

7. Mr and Mrs Busy have invited friends to dinner on the third Friday in July. **What date is that?** _____ Draw a plate of nice food in the correct box.

8. The family are going on holidays for two weeks on 21st July. **Bob will miss football training and Barbara will miss dancing lessons. What dates will they miss?** _____, _____, _____, _____

159

How long?

Record the times for some of your activities.

1. I got up at _____ this morning. I arrived at school at _____.
   How much time had passed from when you got up until you arrived
   at school? _____ mins

2. Pick any lesson with your teacher today. Time the lesson from
   start to finish. **The lesson lasted** _____

3. My morning break lasts _____ minutes. Lunch break
   lasts _____ minutes. That is _____ minutes in all.

4. Time your journey home from school today. **My journey home
   took** _____ minutes.

5. See how long it takes you to do your homework and write the
   length of time here. _____

6. How long do you think it takes Mam or Dad to prepare the evening
   meal? _____. Now find out how long it really takes. _____

7. I watched television for _____ hr _____ mins this evening.

8. See if you can work out about how many hours you sleep at night.
   I go to bed at _____. I get up at _____.
   I usually sleep for _____ hours.

You need:
- colouring pencils   - ruler
- to explain 'pictogram', 'block graphs' and 'bar charts'

1. This bag contains 5 black, 3 yellow, 5 orange, 8 red and 4 blue counters. Draw the correct numbers of coloured counters into this pictogram. The first line is done for you.

black counters	● ● ● ● ●
yellow counters	
red counters	
blue counters	
orange counters	

Now answer these questions.
(a) How many yellow counters? _____
(b) How many more red counters than blue counters? _____
(c) How many blue and orange counters altogether? _____
(d) How many counters in all in the bag? _____

2. A group of children were asked to choose their favourite fruit from this list: bananas, apples, oranges, grapes or peaches.
This pictogram shows the results.

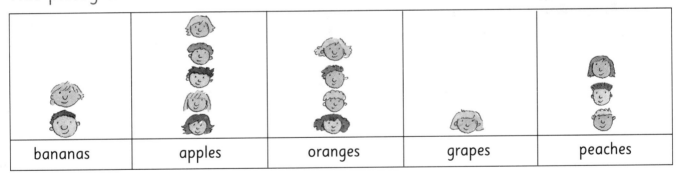

| bananas | apples | oranges | grapes | peaches |

(a) Which was the most popular fruit? _____
(b) Which was the least popular fruit? _____
(c) How many children chose peaches? _____
(d) How many more children chose apples than bananas? _____
(e) How many children were in the group? _____

3. Your teacher will help you to ask your class to choose their favourite fruit from the list in Question 2. Draw a pictogram in your copy to show the results.

Block graphs

1. Ms O'Connor asked the pupils in her class to choose which pet they would like from this list: cat, pony, dog, hamster or goldfish. This block graph shows the results.

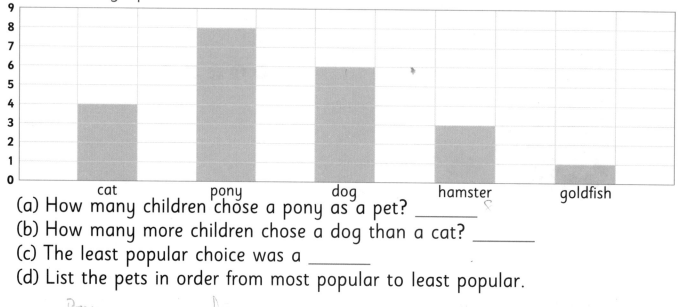

(a) How many children chose a pony as a pet? _____

(b) How many more children chose a dog than a cat? _____

(c) The least popular choice was a _____

(d) List the pets in order from most popular to least popular.

___Pony___ ___Dog___ _____ _____ _____

2.  Ms Carroll is secretary of a big school. The pupils in third class asked her to keep a note of the number of letters delivered to the school on each of the five days of one week. Here is what she wrote.

Monday: 7   Tuesday: 5   Wednesday: 3   Thursday: 1   Friday: 6

Finish this block graph to show the number of letters delivered each day.

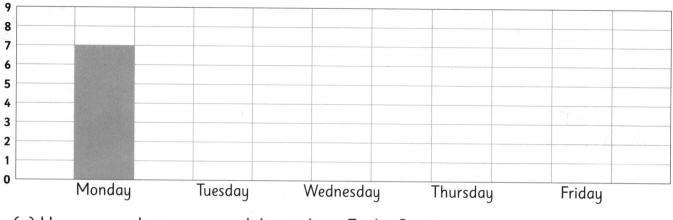

(a) How many letters were delivered on Friday? _____

(b) How many more letters were delivered on Monday than on Wednesday? _____

(c) How many letters were delivered to the school that week? _____

Bar charts

Peter was waiting for his Dad at the door of the hardware shop. His teacher had said that he was to collect information and draw a bar chart as homework. He had a bright idea. He asked his Dad for some paper and a pencil and he collected information about the different coloured cars in the car park. Here is the bar chart he drew as homework.

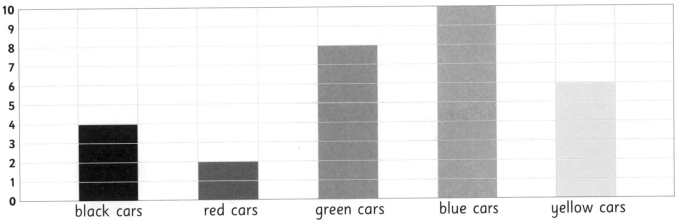

Look at numbers 0 to 10 on the left hand side of the bar chart.
Peter drew the bar for the black cars up as far as the number 4,
so he counted 4 black cars in the car park.
How many blue cars did he count? _____

(a) How many more blue cars than black cars did Peter see? _____

(b) There were only _____ red cars in the car park.

(c) There were twice as many green cars as _____ cars.

(d) There were twice as many black cars as _____ cars.

(e) There were _____ less yellow cars than green cars in the car park.

(f) How many cars were in the car park altogether? _____

(g) Write out the number of cars of each colour starting with the greatest.

_____   _____   _____   _____   _____

More bar charts

1. Mrs Cassidy, the principal of St Patrick's School, was having the school painted. She asked every child in the school to vote on the colour for the front door. Here are the results.

colour	yellow	brown	green	blue	red
number of votes	20	35	45	30	50

Mrs Cassidy made a bar chart so that everyone could see the results. Instead of using a very long piece of paper to show these big numbers she worked in groups of five. Look at her bar chart.

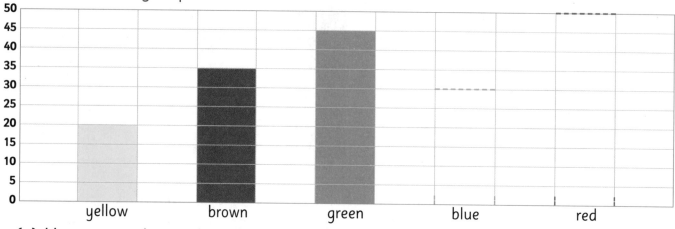

(a) Use your ruler and pencil to complete the bar chart.

(b) How many children were in the school on the day of the vote? _____

(c) What colour was chosen for the school door? _____

2. Your teacher will help you to gather the information you now need from your class.

Our Favourite Television Programmes

programme					
number of children					

Our Favourite Sports

sport					
number of children					

3. Now draw a block graph and a bar chart for
    (a) the favourite television programmes (b) the favourite sports for your class.

4. Discuss with your teacher what information you would like to collect. When you have the information, draw a block graph or a bar chart in your copy to show your findings.

1. Find the missing numbers.

(a) 5 + ___ = 9   (b) 6 + ___ = 12   (c) 9 + ___ = 17

(d) 10 + ___ = 23   (e) 11 + ___ = 32   (f) 24 + ___ = 40

2. Try these.

(a) 24 + ___ = 52   (b) 47 + ___ = 72   (c) 56 + ___ = 91

Even though there is an addition (+) sign it may be easier to get the answer by subtraction.

Let's do Questions (a), (b) and (c) above again using subtraction.

(a)
$$\begin{array}{r} {}^{4}\!\!\not{5}{}^{1}\!2 \\ -\ 24 \\ \hline 28 \end{array}$$

(b)
$$\begin{array}{r} {}^{6}\!\!\not{7}{}^{1}\!2 \\ -\ 47 \\ \hline 25 \end{array}$$

(c)
$$\begin{array}{r} {}^{8}\!\!\not{9}{}^{1}\!1 \\ -\ 56 \\ \hline 35 \end{array}$$

3. Now find the missing numbers in the following questions by subtraction.

(a) 62 + ___ = 91
$$\begin{array}{r} 91 \\ -\ 62 \\ \hline \end{array}$$

(b) 214 + ___ = 323
$$\begin{array}{r} - \\ \hline \end{array}$$

(c) 48 + ___ = 86
$$\begin{array}{r} 86 \\ -\ 48 \\ \hline \end{array}$$

(d) 298 + ___ = 462
$$\begin{array}{r} - \\ \hline \end{array}$$

(e) 142 + ___ = 251
$$\begin{array}{r} 251 \\ -\ 142 \\ \hline \end{array}$$

(f) 432 + ___ = 600
$$\begin{array}{r} - \\ \hline \end{array}$$

(g) 151 + ___ = 311
$$\begin{array}{r} 311 \\ -\ 151 \\ \hline \end{array}$$

(h) 628 + ___ = 901
$$\begin{array}{r} - \\ \hline \end{array}$$

Magic squares

1. The magic number is 15. Find the missing numbers.

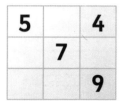

(a) 4 + ___ + 7 = 15
(b) 4 + ___ + 3 = 15
(c) 7 + ___ + 6 = 15
(d) 3 + ___ + 6 = 15

You could also find the missing number in the frame at (a) like this:
15 − (4 + 7) = 4
Can you now find the missing numbers in (b), (c) and (d) in the same way?

2. Now see if you can complete this magic square. The magic number is ____

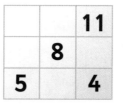

(a) __8__ + ___ + __7__ = 18   __18__ − (__8__ + 7) = ___
(b) ___ + ___ + ___ = 18   ___ − (___ + ___) = ___
(c) ___ + ___ + ___ = ___   ___ − (___ + ___) = ___
(d) ___ + ___ + ___ = ___   ___ − (___ + ___) = ___

3. Complete the magic squares.

5		4
	7	
		9

Magic number is ___

		11
	8	
5		4

Magic number is ___

8		
13	10	7

Magic number is ___

4. Now make up 3 magic squares of your own.

Magic number is ___

Magic number is ___

Magic number is ___

Multiply or divide

1. Put in the missing numbers.

   (a) 2 x ___ = 8   (b) 2 x ___ = 12   (c) 2 x ___ = 20   (d) 8 x ___ = 40

   (e) 3 x ___ = 12   (f) 4 x ___ = 20   (g) 5 x ___ = 45   (h) 9 x ___ = 63

   (i) 6 x ___ = 48   (j) 7 x ___ = 21   (k) 8 x ___ = 72   (l) 7 x ___ = 56

2. Try these.

   (a) 2 x ___ = 36   (b) 3 x ___ = 45   (c) 4 x ___ = 68   (d) 5 x ___ = 80

Even though there is a multiplication sign (x) in these 3 questions, it may be easier to get the answer by division.

Let's do Question (a), (b) and (c) above using division.

(a) $2\overline{|3^16}$ (b) $3\overline{|4^15}$ (c) $4\overline{|6^28}$ (d) $5\overline{|8^30}$
       18   15   17   16

3. Now find the missing numbers in the following questions by division.
   The first one is done for you.

   (a) 2 x **25** = 50 $2\overline{|5^10}$ (b) 2 x ___ = 62 $2\overline{|62}$
                            25   ___

   (c) 3 x ___ = 75 $3\overline{|75}$ (d) 4 x ___ = 80 $4\overline{|80}$
                            ___   ___

   (e) 5 x ___ = 90 $5\overline{|90}$ (f) 5 x ___ = 100 $5\overline{|100}$
                            ___   ___

   (g) 6 x ___ = 108 $6\overline{|108}$ (h) 6 x ___ = 108 $6\overline{|108}$
                            ___   ___

   (i) 4 x ___ = 128 $4\overline{|128}$ (j) 8 x ___ = 200 $8\overline{|200}$
                            ___   ___

Number sentences

When we write an English story we use words and sentences, but in mathematics we can tell a story with numbers and symbols. Look at this word sentence.

Mary bought six sweets in the shop on Monday and bought nine more on Tuesday. So she bought fifteen sweets altogether on the two days.

You can write this word story in mathematics like this: $6 + 9 = 15$
We call it a number sentence.

1. Write a number sentence for each of these stories
    (a) Aoife spent 23c in the shop yesterday and 46c the
    day before. She spent 69c altogether.   ___ + ___ = ___

    (b) Joan collected 16 stamps and her big sister gave
    her another 48 stamps. She had 64 stamps altogether.   ___ + ___ = ___

    (c) Martin's Dad won a prize of €50 but he bought a
    shirt for €39. He now had €11 left.   ___ + ___ = ___

There is a piece of information missing in this story:

There are 36 apples in one box and 14 in another. How many apples are there altogether? ___
The number sentence to match this story is 36 + 14 = ___

2. Write number sentences to match these stories and find the answers.
    (a) There are 32 pupils in third class and 29 in fourth class.
    How many pupils altogether in the two classes?   ___ + ___ = ___

    (b) Fiona had 35c to buy a copy at school but she lost 20c of
    it on the way to school. How much money did she have left? ___ + ___ = ___

    (c) Aisling has a CD rack that holds 75 CDs. She has
    48 CDs at the moment.
    How many more does she need to buy to fill the rack?   ___ + ___ = ___

Matching

Below are 6 number sentences with 6 word stories to match them.
Match each word story with the correct number sentence.
Then find the answers.

Number sentences

(a) $(3 \times 7) + 5 =$ (b) $(3 + 7) - 5 =$

(c) $(5 + 7) \div 2 =$ (d) $(5 \times 3) - 7 =$

(e) $(5 + 20) - 8 =$ (f) $(3 + 7) \div 2 =$

Word stories

1. Deirdre has 5 stickers and Sinéad has 7. They decided to share them equally between them. How many did each have then? _____

2. Yesterday Thomas had 3 black marbles and 7 green ones. On the way home from school he gave 5 of them to his best friend Liam. How many had he left? _____

3. Martha had 3 sweets and Paula had 7 sweets. They agreed to share them equally between them. How many did each have then? _____

4. Anne had a 5c coin and a 20c coin. She spent 8c. How much had she left? _____

5. Mammy, Daddy, Aunt Dolly and Paul went on a train journey. The adults' tickets cost €7 while Paul's cost €5. How much does the train journey cost altogether? _____

6. I had 5 packs of pens with 3 pens in each pack. I sold 7 pens. How many had I left? ___

Number sentence (a) matches word story _____

Number sentence (b) matches word story _____

Number sentence (c) matches word story _____

Number sentence (d) matches word story _____

Number sentence (e) matches word story _____

Number sentence (f) matches word story _____

Chapter 39

A long look back

1. 684 + 93 + 7 + 560 = _____

2. 836 + 9 + 74 + 126 = _____

3. 123 – 86 = _____

4. 903 – 168 = _____

5. 5 x 9 = _____

6. 8 x 7 = _____

7. 4 x 9 = _____

8. 3 x 9 = _____

9. 7 x _____ = 42

10.
```
  28
x  4
————
————
```

11.
```
  36
x  6
————
————
```

12.
```
  48
x  7
————
————
```

13. 45 ÷ 5 = _____

14. 63 ÷ 7 = _____

15. 42 ÷ 6 = _____

16. 42 ÷ 3 = _____

17. 4 ⌐72

18. 8 ⌐184

19. 4 ⌐53

20. 9 ⌐194

Fill in the missing fractions on the number lines.

21.
```
0     1/4    1/2    ___    1
```

22.
```
0   1/8   1/4   ___   1/2   5/8   3/4   7/8   1
```

23. $\frac{1}{4}$ of 28 = __

24. $\frac{1}{8}$ of 160 = __

25. 0.5 = $\boxed{\frac{}{2}}$

26. Colour 0.3 of this shape:

27. What time is it?

28. Paula arrived home from school at ten minutes to three in the afternoon. Show the time on this digital watch.

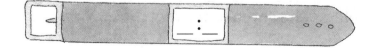

29. How much money is in this purse?

€_____._____

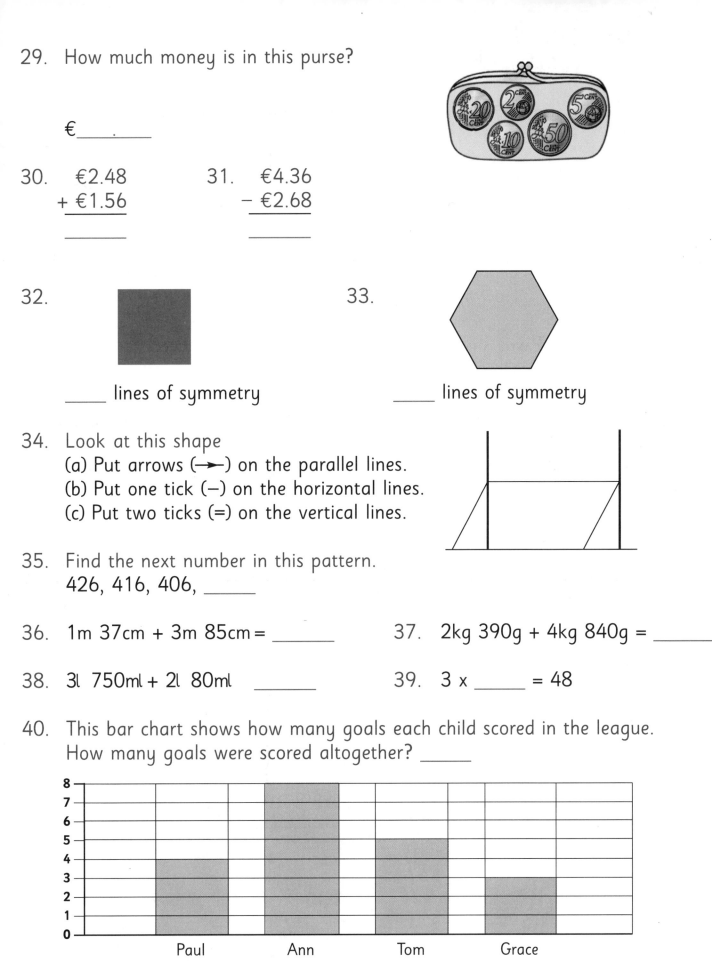

30. €2.48
   + €1.56
   _____

31. €4.36
   − €2.68
   _____

32. _____ lines of symmetry

33. _____ lines of symmetry

34. Look at this shape
    (a) Put arrows (→) on the parallel lines.
    (b) Put one tick (−) on the horizontal lines.
    (c) Put two ticks (=) on the vertical lines.

35. Find the next number in this pattern.
    426, 416, 406, _____

36. 1m 37cm + 3m 85cm = _____

37. 2kg 390g + 4kg 840g = _____

38. 3l 750ml + 2l 80ml _____

39. 3 x _____ = 48

40. This bar chart shows how many goals each child scored in the league.
    How many goals were scored altogether? _____

41. There are 24 pencils in a box. How many pencils in 8 boxes? _____

42. Aisling bought an ice-cream for 65c and a magazine for €1.68. How much did she spend altogether? _____

43. How much heavier is a ham that weighs 4k 165g than a chicken that weighs 2kg 280g? _____

44.  Paula and Emma collected 96 conkers between them last year. They gave a $\frac{1}{4}$ of them to their best friend Michelle. How many did they give to Michelle? _____

45. A prize of €45 was shared equally among three people. How much did each person get? _____

46.  The Dublin to Cork train had 405 passengers on board when it left Heuston Station. 129 people got off at Thurles and nobody got on. How many were still on the train? _____

47. When I rolled 2 dice I scored 13. Do you think that is
    (a) possible? ☐   (b) impossible? ☐   Put a tick (✓) in the correct box.

48. Ciara has 96 marbles but her friend Mary has 48 more than her. How many marbles does Mary have? _____

49. There are 24 hours in a day. How many hours in a week? _____

50. Mr Dunne bought 6 kitchen chairs. He paid a total of €150 for them. How much is that per chair? _____

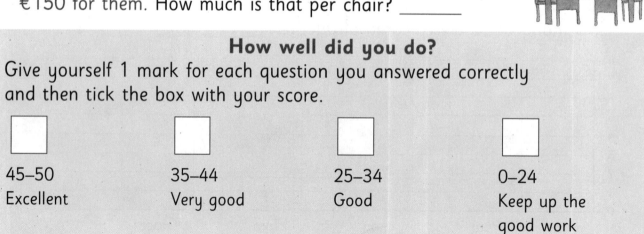

How well did you do?

Give yourself 1 mark for each question you answered correctly and then tick the box with your score.

☐ 45–50 Excellent   ☐ 35–44 Very good   ☐ 25–34 Good   ☐ 0–24 Keep up the good work